CONTEMPORARY PLAYWRIGHTS
JOHN WHITING

CONTEMPORARY PLAYWRIGHTS

JOHN WHITING
BY
RONALD HAYMAN

HEINEMANN · LONDON

Heinemann Educational Books Ltd
London Edinburgh Melbourne Toronto
Singapore Auckland Johannesburg
Ibadan Hong Kong Nairobi

ISBN 0 435 18431 8 (cased edition)
ISBN 0 435 18406 7 (paperback)

Published by Heinemann Educational Books Ltd
48 Charles Street, London W1X 8AH
Printed in Great Britain by
Cox & Wyman Ltd, London, Fakenham and Reading

CONTENTS

ACKNOWLEDGEMENTS

The author would like to thank Mrs Gabrielle Scott Robinson of Urbana University, Illinois, for letting him read the Ph.D thesis she wrote on John Whiting for London University and letting him make use of her compendious bibliography in compiling his.

The photographs of *A Penny for a Song* are reproduced by courtesy of Dominic; that of *The Devils* by courtesy of Reg Wilson; that of *Marching Song* by courtesy of Angus McBean Ltd.

JOHN WHITING

Texts

The Collected Plays of John Whiting (Vols. I & II), Heinemann
  Educational Books 1969

The Plays of John Whiting (Saint's Day, A Penny for a Song and
  Marching Song), William Heinemann 1957

Saint's Day. Plays of the Year, Vol. 6, 1951, ed. J. C. Trewin. Elek
  1952, Heinemann Educational Books 1963, Hereford Plays Series
  with an introduction by E. R. Wood

A Penny for a Song (revised version), Heinemann Educational Books
  1964, Hereford Plays Series with an introduction by E. R. Wood

Marching Song, Samuel French 1964; Heinemann Educational Books
  1962, Hereford Plays Series with an introduction by E. R. Wood

Ring Up the Curtain, William Heinemann 1955, Heinemann Educational Books 1962

  New English Dramatists 5, Penguin Plays 1962

No Why, in *The London Magazine* May 1961

  Samuel French 1961

The Devils, William Heinemann 1961

  New English Dramatists 6, Penguin Plays 1963

Collected Criticism

John Whiting on Theatre London Magazine Editions. Alan Ross 1966

Select Bibliography of (a) articles by Whiting
                       (b) articles on Whiting

(a) 'Writing for Actors', *The Adelphi*, 2nd Quarter 1952

  'A Conversation', *Nimbus*, June–August 1953

  'What the Theatre Means to Me', *Plays and Players*, August 1954

  'The Toll of Talent in a Timid Theatre', *Encore*, Summer 1956

  'From a Notebook', *The International Theatre Annual*, No. 1

John Whiting

'A Writer's Prospect – V, The Writer's Theatre', *The London Magazine*, December 1956

'The Art of the Dramatist', *Plays and Players*, November 1957

'At Ease in a Bright Red Tie', *Encore*, September–October 1959

'Writer as Gangster'. An Interview, *Encore*, January–February 1961

'From My Diary', *Twentieth Century*, February 1961

(b) Adler, Henry	'Wanamaker and Whiting', *Encore*, November–December 1957
Cairns, Adrian	'The Significance of John Whiting's Plays', *International Theatre Annual*, No. 1
Ferman, James and Hall, Peter	'John Whiting, un nouvel auteur dramatique anglais', *La Revue des Lettres Modernes*, août–sept. 1954
Hayman, Ronald	'Marching Song and John Whiting', *Nimbus*, Autumn 1954
Milne, Tom	'The Hidden Face of Violence', *Encore*, January–February 1960
O'Connor, Garry	'The Obsessions of John Whiting', *Encore*, July–August 1964
Trussler, Simon	'The Plays of John Whiting', *Tulane Drama Review*, Winter 1966

Performances

March 1951	*A Penny for a Song* at the Haymarket, directed by Peter Brook, with Alan Webb, Ronald Squire, Virginia McKenna and Ronald Howard
September 1951	*Saint's Day* at the Arts Theatre, directed by Stephen Murray, with Michael Hordern and Valerie White
February 1954	*Marching Song* at the St Martin's, directed by Frith Banbury, with Robert Flemyng, Diana Wynyard, Penelope Munday, Hartley Power and Ernest Thesiger

Bibliography

January 1955	*Marching Song* at the Düsseldorfer Schauspielhaus, directed by Gustaf Gründgens
August 1956	*The Gates of Summer* at the Oxford Playhouse, directed by Peter Hall, with James Donald, Dorothy Tutin, Isabel Jeans and Lionel Jeffries
February 1961	*The Devils* at the Aldwych, directed by Peter Wood, with Richard Johnson and Dorothy Tutin
August 1962	*A Penny for a Song* at the Aldwych (revised version), directed by Colin Graham, with Marius Goring, Michael Gwynn, Judi Dench and Mark Eden
July 1964	*No Why* at the Aldwych, directed by John Schlesinger, with Derek Godfrey
May 1965	*Saint's Day* at Stratford East, directed by David Jones, with Michael Hordern and Sheila Allen
October 1965	*Conditions of Agreement* at the Little Theatre, Bristol, directed by Christopher Denys

JOHN WHITING

When twenty-first-century critics look back at our twentieth-century playwrights, how will they assess the work of John Whiting? Already, the sixties have been far kinder to his work than the fifties. In 1951 Alec Clunes, Peter Ustinov, and Christopher Fry, judges in the Arts Theatre's Festival of Britain Play Competition, awarded the first prize to *Saint's Day* – in the teeth of the critics who had all savaged it. Several of them said it was the worst of the three plays which had been picked out of the thousand entries for a week's trial run at the Arts. Tyrone Guthrie, Peter Brook, Peggy Ashcroft, and John Gielgud wrote letters to *The Times* in defence of the play but it didn't get a revival until June 1965 when Stage Sixty presented it at Stratford East. *A Penny for a Song*, which was written later, had already been presented in the West End earlier in 1951, and had a very short run, despite a production by Peter Brook and designs by Emmett. It's since been revived at the Aldwych (August 1962) and made into an opera with music by Richard Rodney Bennett (Sadler's Wells, 1967). *Marching Song* ran for five and a half weeks at the St Martin's in 1954 and it's still waiting for a revival, as is Whiting's comedy *The Gates of Summer*, which collapsed on what was meant to be a pre-London tour in 1956. *The Devils*, though it's not such a good play as *Saint's Day* or *Marching Song*, was much more successful with both critics and audiences when the Royal Shakespeare Company put it on at the Aldwych in February 1961 as the third play in their first season there. *Conditions of Agreement*, Whiting's first play, written in 1946, didn't get a production till October 1965, when the Bristol Old Vic put it on at their Little Theatre.

Why have Whiting's plays never caught on at the box office? Words like 'obscurity', 'coldness', 'remoteness' are usually used against them, but the comedies have enormous charm while the tragedies have enormous power. They really deserve to be called tragedies and they have heroes in them who deserve to be called heroes. But Whiting makes enormous demands on his public and his plays could only have succeeded if an audience had been created for

1

John Whiting

them, as it was for Beckett's and Pinter's. If the Royal Court had existed in the early fifties, and if it had taken up Whiting's cause (which it didn't even in the late fifties) it's quite possible that he could have become fashionable.

His plays are quite unlike anyone else's. They fit into no movement, no category. But they belong very much together, constituting a corpus of original, distinguished and highly stylish writing for the theatre. In a lot of ways, they're very unlike each other but they have more in common than the high quality of the writing. The dialogue is incisive, arresting, dense, modulating easily from an elegant literariness to colloquial terseness and he was an excellent story-teller in theatrical terms, good at interweaving the threads in his action and at keeping us fascinated by what's happening, hungry to know what's going to happen next.

At the beginning of the fifties many people believed in the possibility of a renaissance of verse drama, putting their faith in T. S. Eliot and Christopher Fry as the playwrights who could save the English Theatre from the creeping paralysis of naturalism. But nothing Eliot wrote for the theatre was as dramatic as *Sweeney Agonistes*, *The Rock* choruses, and *Murder in the Cathedral*. As a poet he was capable of great drama but as a dramatist his development was a steady decline. Whiting was himself among those who overrated Christopher Fry and there are passages, particularly in *A Penny for a Song*, where the Fry influence has rubbed off, while Stella's 'point of deviation' speech in *Saint's Day* is a deliberate piece of Eliot pastiche. (When he wrote *Saint's Day*, he didn't think it stood any chance of being staged.)

> STELLA (*she cries out*): Then what is going to happen? (*There is a complete cessation of activity whilst* STELLA *speaks. She is swept by a sudden storm of fore-knowledge, awful in its clarity. The men, silent and unmoving, watch her.*) Careful! We are approaching the point of deviation. At one moment there is laughter and conversation and a progression: people move and speak smoothly and casually, their breathing is controlled and they know what they do. Then there occurs a call from another room, the realization that a member of the assembly is missing, the sudden shout into the dream and the waking to find the body with the failing heart lying in the corridor –

> with the twisted limbs at the foot of the stairs – the man
> hanging from the beam, or the child floating drowned in the
> garden pool. Careful! Be careful! We are approaching that
> point. The moment of the call from another room. (*She pauses.*)
> Give me another of your cigarettes, Paul.

But altogether, Whiting succeeded in doing in prose what Eliot and
Fry were failing to do in verse. He discovered the secret, which eluded
them, of investing his characters with a significance equal to that of
what they say. Eliot's imagery is often very exciting on a verbal level
but it never ignites theatrically because the personalities never
become as compelling as the language. The uncles and aunts in *The
Family Reunion* are fine when they coalesce into a chorus but dreary
stereotypes when they speak as individuals. In *Murder in the Cathedral*
Beckett is rather like a chorus because he refuses to become a protagonist – he lets God's Word speak through him. But Harry, the
hero of *The Family Reunion*, has to make his own decisions, and his
actions lag behind his language. Eliot's insistence on the inadequacy
of the individual consciousness was a great barrier to creating
interesting personalities in his characters. Whiting makes his characters highly conscious, highly articulate, and highly exciting. Many
of them are capable of stepping outside themselves to talk like a
chorus on their own situation, but they never go 'out of character'
or lose their individuality in doing so:

Whiting also knew how to integrate his imagery into his action.
What Stella prophesies is going to happen, horribly: the call from
another room is not just a verbal image. And the antique helmet on
a plinth, which is a visual image in *Marching Song* – part of the set –
becomes a verbal image in Rupert's speeches and also becomes
relevant to the working out of the relationships in the action.

Whiting always plants his images in soil which will make them
flower dramatically, but part of the reason they acquire such resonance for us is that they had so much for him, coming as they do from
what he called his private mythology:

> The most dangerous tendency of modern criticism towards the
> work of young writers, especially in the theatre, is that it sets out
> to destroy by ridicule or abuse the writer's private mythology.

3

John Whiting

Yet it is this private world which prevents the play becoming mere bombast, or journalism. If we are normal human beings we live surrounded by terrors, clowns, dead loves and old fears, represented by, say, a painting on a wall, some reels of photographic negative, a rose garden and a call from another room. The artist, admitting their significance, naturally reaches out for them in the desperate emergency of creation. They are nothing in themselves, these material things, but what they evoke for us as writers matters very much. Certainly if we fail to communicate this to an audience it demonstrates our failure as artists. But the fact that we use them does not demonstrate our failure as men, as is so often implied.

Many of the long speeches in Whiting's plays are there partly to explicate the dramatic meaning of these images. Today we've grown quite accustomed to long speeches from the work of Osborne, Beckett, Pinter, and Arden, who all use them, but Whiting was the first playwright in the fifties to dare go to the length in prose that then seemed only acceptable in verse.

When *Conditions of Agreement* was finally staged in 1965, critics like Irving Wardle and Penelope Gilliatt pointed out what a strong foretaste it gave of Pinter. Even today, when we've got used to thinking about how far ahead of his time Whiting was, it's difficult to remember that the year he started writing *Saint's Day* (1947) was the year of *Edward My Son, The Linden Tree, Dr Angelus, Peace in Our Time, Deep Are the Roots, Oklahoma, Annie Get Your Gun,* and *Bless the Bride.*

CONDITIONS OF AGREEMENT

It's hard to see *Conditions of Agreement* for what it really is in itself: so many themes are announced in it which Whiting was later to develop more adroitly, so many images and preoccupations which later recur more forcefully. The dialogue is sometimes colloquial and sparse, almost like Pinter, sometimes literary and deliberate, almost like Ivy Compton Burnett. 'It is my precaution always to type the envelopes,' says Peter Bembo, an ex-circus clown. And, 'Probably my signature lacked uniformity because my life lacked stability'. The battles for territory are Pinteresque too and there's a scene of verbal bullying with two men sharing their lines as they converge on their victim, just as Goldberg and McCann do in *The Birthday Party* as they converge on Stanley.

> PETER (*to* A.G.): You are in great danger.
> NICHOLAS: Yes.
> PETER: You must behave naturally however.
> NICHOLAS: We —
> PETER: Casually.
> NICHOLAS: The situation calls —
> PETER: You must not – *must not* betray the slightest anxiety or fear.
> NICHOLAS: I agree.
> PETER: You must laugh. Be – be —
> NICHOLAS: Devil-may-care.
> PETER: But I do not.
> (PETER *and* NICHOLAS *laugh*.)
> Yes. That is how you must behave.
> NICHOLAS: Better?
> PETER: Feel better, A.G.?
> NICHOLAS: Well enough to discuss our plans? For we have plans to help you. Haven't we, Peter?
> PETER: We have.
> NICHOLAS: Yes, you look better. Listen to me. Can you hear me? (*To* PETER) Do you think he can hear me?
> PETER (*shouting at* A.G.): Can you hear us?

John Whiting

(A.G. *gives no indication*.)
Yes, he can hear us.

The characters are a very odd collection. The one-eyed Peter has been living in Armenia for the fifteen years since he retired. Returning to England he comes to visit a former girl-friend, Emily Doone, now a widow of fifty-eight living in a small town near Oxford and he invites himself to stay with her. Nicholas, her son, is a one-legged giant of twenty-two who comes back from his honeymoon with his seventeen-year-old wife Patience, who was born illegitimate and grew up in an institution. He treats her like a servant and tells her off for behaving like one. A.G. sounds no more like the retired grocer he is than Peter sounds like an ex-clown. From the beginning Whiting needed to make his characters unnaturalistically articulate about their unnaturalistic self-consciousness. When Dido in *Marching Song* says 'I'm the girl you see on the edge of the crowd at a street accident', this is the pithy end-result of writing four plays in which characters have commented on themselves as if from outside.

The writing in *Conditions of Agreement* is more diffuse than in Whiting's later plays. Nearly all his characters have time on their hands and this in itself makes for leisureliness but in the later plays the action is always keyed up by preparations for events they're expecting. Here nothing of any moment is expected to happen and the plans Peter and Nicholas make against A.G. in Act Two are very vague. The play is like Ibsen's and unlike Pinter's in that the plot depends fairly heavily on past action and Act One is very slow in digging it out of the past. A.G.'s wife died during a circus performance in Spain while the crowd was watching Peter. So the old clown's boast, 'There was never a tear shed except of laughter' is contradicted by A.G.'s story. Although the narrative line is shared in most of these conversations which resurrect the past, the effect is more often lyrical than dramatic, even when the rhetoric has a sour sting in its tail, as in this description of the charity dance for crippled children where Emily and Peter met:

> PETER: 'This is Miss Emily Heitland, one of our committee,' she said.

EMILY: And you said, 'How d'you do', and stood on your head. Your trousers slipped down to your knees and showed your yellow socks. I stood before you, your face at my feet, with my hand stretched out like a fool. All around us the children laughed and clattered their little wooden legs.

Nor had Whiting yet developed his remarkable dexterity at getting characters on and off stage, so a good deal of dialogue is wasted over insignificant and fairly boring details like the reading lamp Nicholas has made for A.G. But there are also moments, which stand out as extremely theatrical, as when A.G., under the misapprehension that Peter is deaf, abruptly shouts at him, 'Who are you? What are you doing here?'

A.G. remembers Bembo the Clown, but thought he was dead, just as people think Paul Southman is dead, and Dido thinks Rupert Forster is dead. (Peter's long stay in Armenia is never explained but he's the first of Whiting's many exiles.) His morbid curiosity about the incident in which someone wept at one of his performances, as A.G. did when his wife died, cues a detailed account of what happened – the first piece of sustained narrative in Whiting. He succeeds in winding the scene up to considerable tension, which depends partly on the co-presence of comic and tragic elements in the crucial moment of the past. The crowd went on laughing at Peter's antics while the distressed husband, unable to speak the language, shouted out to them to help his wife, who was hanging upside down with her heel caught in the structure of the stand and her skirts falling over her head.

Much of the behaviour in *Conditions of Agreement* is quite unrealistic. Peter's exaggerated concern about whether A.G. wept there and then or not until afterwards could only be explained if the boast about 'never a tear, except of laughter' were a kind of life-line to him, as the goat-song is to Rupert, and when Nicholas and Patience arrive, everyone behaves very oddly, though the oddness is certainly theatrical. A.G. leaves immediately and Patience, although obviously dominated by her husband, disobeys him when he gives her an order which would take her out of the room.

Nicholas's strained relationship with his mother also generates tension and he talks sardonically to Patience about her ex-lovers:

John Whiting

NICHOLAS: You will find, Patience, that we are often attended by elderly gentlemen with a kind of fading love-light in their eyes.

EMILY: Shut up!

NICHOLAS: They will be introduced and explained to you by Mother as, 'A very old friend of mine. I knew him many years ago – before you were born'. That formula introduces each one. There was Harry or Henry or whatever his name was – ten years ago when I was still a child – Harry died but he didn't leave us any of his money. Then there was Andrew – one of the hearty kind – he used to frighten me – he died but he didn't leave us any money: it wasn't until after he was dead that we found he hadn't any money to leave, was it, Emmy? There were others in varying stages of wealth and penury. All acquaintances of my mother until she met my father and became respectable. I must say she still appears to possess great charm.

When Patience and Nicholas are left alone, the difficulty she has in picturing Emily and Peter as young and capable of making love is amusing in itself and helps to create the kind of perspective gap between the generations that Whiting always liked to sketch in. Most of his plays have at least one scene with an old man talking to a child or a young girl.

Then comes one of the rare moments of reciprocated passion in his plays.

PATIENCE: There is no cause to be afraid of the night. Why are you shy with me? You must have no shame with me. Together, we must be gay and impudent – and it must be you who comes to me to demand and be bold. I want that.

The lyricism in Patience's appeal is rather like that in Stella's appeal to Charles in *Saint's Day*. Even the cadences are feminine. But the flow of the rhetoric is immediately checked as she steps back from him, and from herself.

I had to say that.

And within less than a minute, Nicholas, who is obsessed by money and writes down each day's expenses in a notebook, is lecturing her about spending too much.

Nicholas's hatred of A.G. seems to be founded more on jealousy of his money than on jealousy of Emily's liking for him, and Peter's hostility to the retired grocer seems to be based, even more quirkily, on the blow A.G. has dealt to his professional pride. But it's the enmity which is important, not the reasons for it. Act One ends menacingly with Nicholas and the women laughing at Peter, who is wearing a false nose, while he talks over the telephone to A.G., with a false friendliness in his voice, telling him to come over. In Act Two the one-eyed old clown and the one-legged young husband join forces against the harmless old man, plotting against him as if they were planning a military operation. (The imagery of warfare is very important in Whiting's work and all his plays, except *No Why*, have soldiers at least mentioned in them, if they don't actually appear. In *Conditions of Agreement*, Emily is the widow of a soldier.)

A.G. is a natural victim because he's old and alone. His scene with Emily shows that he's not in love with her but depends on her for human contact. It's the birthday of his dead wife (birthdays are also important for Whiting) and he wants Emily to accept her ivory prayer book as a present. Like Rupert in *Marching Song* who could take no initiative after ordering the massacre of the children, A.G. has been arrested by the moment of his wife's death. He can't forget it and he can't get beyond it. He talks about it compulsively and the play tries to show the difficulty he has in translating the things which have private significance for him into gestures which have meaning for other people. Emily doesn't want to accept the gift but she goes out with him to the church.

The first verbal onslaught is made in his absence, as Nicholas and Peter watch him and Emily through the window. The sardonic style is now possible for them because they have each other as allies.

> There they go. That strut of A.G.'s is more comic seen from the rear. I want you to observe the angle of his hat – jaunty, I believe is the term. Notice the swing of the cane – Yes, look! A full circle. Ah! He tips his hat to an acquaintance. (*Mimics.*) 'How d'you do. How d'you do.' (*He pauses.*) And note, please, Peter, Emmy's grace.

John Whiting

Paul plays to Charles rather like this in *Saint's Day*, especially in the scene with Aldus, and what Nicholas and Peter want to do is destroy A.G.'s innocence, rather as Paul and Charles destroy Procathren's.

> Since Thursday, when you came here, you have been angry and defiant – only too willing to discuss the A.G. affair with me. It's true we made no definite plans but you were loud in your support of anything I might do – anything. You remember you definitely offered me your co-operation. Until last night you were malicious and violent towards A.G. It was only last night you said of A.G., 'It is his innocence we must destroy,' and, you said, 'That cannot be achieved by intimidation,' and then you yawned and went to bed saying we'd discuss it further this morning. Here is this morning and you are taking my conjectures, my attempts at a solution to our problem, my tentative, inexperienced efforts to put A.G. in his rightful place and you are laughing at them – and, I suppose, at me.

A parallel is clearly intended, but not quite substantiated, with the destruction of Nicholas's innocence by Patience. His bedroom still has a cupboard in it full of toys and there are still childhood books on the shelves. Patience violates this when she clears them away to make space for the dresses Emily has given her. (She appears in one of them, as in *Marching Song* Dido appears in one belonging to Catherine's maid.) Nicholas is furious and hits her across the face but the real reasons for his resentment are clear from his denunciation of her to Peter:

> The girl has degraded me beyond expectation. I was prepared as a necessity of marriage to give myself to a degree but she has made me debase myself until – I – don't – sucking at – in the violence of – look at her hands, you look — Before, I'd only limited knowledge – walking home through the park at night I had seen the couples linked on benches, lying among bushes, plucking at each other's clothing in an aimless passion like dying people. Even the sight of this attacked my – my – yes, innocence. Yes! my innocence. Now this girl, my wife, has made me — My bedroom which we share has been my refuge for many years.

Just before the curtain of Act Two, as Patience's sobbing dies down, the brass band, which has already been mentioned in Act One, is heard playing. It's nothing like so meaningful or so menacing as the blasts on the trumpet in *Saint's Day* which provide such an excellent curtain for Act One, but it produces something of the same kind of theatrical effect.

The baiting of A.G. starts when Peter trips him and he falls with a teacup in his hand. The pseudo-serious tone of Peter and Nicholas's plotting in his absence is resumed in his presence as they put on a teasing act of helpfulness:

> PETER: We are very distressed. No man likes to be threatened. It is most disturbing. You can be sure of our support and, if necessary, our action against this scoundrel. You have come to us. That is good. It is always to friends you must go in the case of fear.
> (*There is a pause.* A.G. *speaks to* NICHOLAS *and* EMILY.)
> A.G.: The circumstances are these. When we returned from church this morning — (*He pauses and then speaks to* PETER) I am not afraid.

This prefigures the talk of alliances in *Saint's Day*, when Paul and Charles think of forming one with the soldiers against the villagers.

Yet another similarity with *Saint's Day* is that Act Three isn't nearly as good as Acts One and Two. And the main flaw derives from the same mistake of keeping the chief protagonists off-stage for too long, though there's a good twist at the end of the long scene between the two women when Emily tells Patience that what Nicholas is going to do is kill himself. Emily needs Patience (as Catherine needs Dido in *Marching Song*) to save the man from destroying himself. But the play becomes more difficult to follow here.

> If that is his intention you must exercise your strength and surrender yourself to the lack of comprehension that is the blessing of your youth. By attempting to understand you may, by chance, succeed and that will destroy you.

Considerable tension builds up over the threat of suicide, especially when Nicholas is missing from the room. Peter continues the assault

11

against A.G. single-handed, bizarrely pretending to believe that his wife has killed herself.

PETER: But you have implied if not stated so many reasons.

A.G.: Not one!

PETER: One: that she was to remain childless. Two: that she regarded herself as a failure in marriage. Three: that she couldn't live with your kindly reproach. Four: that she was afraid to return to England and a life of boredom with you among the sugar and spices. Five: That she was unbearably moved by the sight of the child coming bravely to me from the audience. Six: that my performance that day was so bad that the poor lady went straight off and did away with herself. Which of these reasons was the actual cause I say I don't know. But you've not only given us reasons – there are the various incidents. Her shoe catching and her hanging head downwards: to give her time for the full realization of the act, do you think? The business of love-making on the preceding night: what other motive had you in telling us that, eh?

The action culminates in a physical attack on A.G., which is cruel and theatrical but after Nicholas's reappearance and the announcement that it was all a joke, it peters from one anticlimax to another, ending disappointingly and indefinitely.

But for a first play it's a remarkable achievement.

SAINT'S DAY

A lot has been written about *Saint's Day* and it's easy to get airborne into abstract discussions of 'meaning' and 'symbolism', snatching themes, images, and statements away from their place in the unfolding action. *Saint's Day* is a complex play which needs – and invites – interpretation, but it's the theatrical experience that matters. The words Whiting wrote are important not as a philosophical riddle but as the score for an elaborate sequence of powerful theatrical effects, which express something complex but coherent, though the 'meaning' can't be translated into a neat explanation. The play only means what it is in performance.

Something of the quality of the theatrical experience is immediately apparent when the curtain goes up. We see a man and a woman standing motionless. The set, the flow of dim light from the oil lamp and from behind the drawn curtains, the disorder in the room, the bicycle in the middle of the floor and the short anxious lines of dialogue which jerk from one subject to another all combine to generate tension and to raise questions without answering them. Something important is going to happen and there is a danger that things will go badly. They don't know whether it's half past eight or half past nine or half past ten. Who are they, where are they and why are they living without a clock that works?

The first two minutes of dialogue are played in the half dark and we don't get oriented at all until Stella pulls back the curtains. As in *Marching Song* we are above ground level. The furniture and the objects in the room are good but neglected. Stella's idea of tidying is to pick up the bicycle pump from the floor and put it on the bicycle. Several hundred books are piled on the floor. A large, garish oil-painting on the wall is still unfinished. The air is full of unanswered questions but the flow of dialogue has firmly established the existence of two characters we haven't yet seen and begun to characterize the two we have: a domineering woman, and a man whose resistance is mainly passive.

13

John Whiting

They are both cold. Why isn't there a fire? The man shouts for John Winter, who doesn't answer. (Who is he? Where is he?) Stella is afraid that the noise will wake Paul but he's already awake and joins in the shouting. The man is concerned about her sickness (Is she pregnant?) and she is worried about Paul's journey. (Why? Who is Paul and where is he going?) We still don't know who Charles is or his relationship to Stella. But we're involved in a definite atmosphere and a well-defined mood of touchy uneasiness.

Stella's scene with John Winter sets the strings of uncertainty throbbing more violently. His position in the household, like his attitude, is ambiguous. He's obviously a servant and they obviously have no money to pay him, but although he stays, they still aren't sure of his loyalty. They depend on him for contact with the village and suspect that his sympathies may be with the hostile villagers. But among its other uses, the figure of John Winter serves as a parody of the Servant, which was almost *de rigueur* in plays of this period. Like Patience (who came nearest to being the servant figure in *Conditions of Agreement*) John Winter isn't always obedient about staying in or going out of the room when told to, but Stella makes him stay to tell him (and us) that Robert Procathren, the well-known poet and critic, is coming to drive Paul to a dinner to be held in his honour in London. Stella wants to offer Robert lunch and she has some difficulty in persuading John Winter to get food from the village, where they already owe so much money to the shopkeepers. This gives her her first speech of any length and it's strikingly less literary than the long speeches in *Conditions of Agreement*. The sentences are short and colloquial with only one piece of phrasing at the end of the speech hich is unconversational.

> Come now, you wouldn't like to see Mr Southman or his guest go without food, would you? Would you? No, of course, you wouldn't, because you love him as I love him, and we'll fight for him, won't we? We'll put our pride in our pocket and we'll fight for him. We've got to look after him, you know. There's no one else. Just you and me, that's all. Now, go along. (CHARLES *comes down the stairs: he is dressed and carries a cup of tea.*) John Winter. (STELLA *goes to* JOHN WINTER *and*

14

puts her arms about him.) John Winter, I want you to go with
my grandfather today – go with him to London – because I
trust you. Remember, he will be among strangers – all his
friends have gone – and he may be frightened. And if he is
afraid he will appear ridiculous. I want you to see that he is
not frightened – that by his age he is great and not ridiculous.
That he is Paul Southman.

WINTER: He is a great and famous man.

Charles's entrance, like so many entrances in Whiting, adds to
the dramatic tension. He's just in time to hear Stella say 'Just you
and me'. He obviously doesn't share her anxiety about getting Paul
to London.

His joke to John Winter, just as the man is going up to Paul,
neatly establishes the existence of the pistol.

He's sitting on his bed cleaning a pistol. You'd better be careful,
John Winter.

A pistol is a very cliché plot requisite but Whiting's use of it is highly
original and whether the threat from the village is real or imagined,
Paul's feelings about it are quite strong enough to justify the presence
of a pistol in the house. Stella is later quite ironic in telling Paul and
Charles off for playing soldiers but she says herself that there was
an evening three years ago when the villagers planned to attack
them but got too drunk to walk the half mile to the house. (Which
plants the distance neatly enough.) And Paul says that if they come,
they will kill him. So *Saint's Day* gives us a much more definite
foretaste than *Conditions of Agreement* of 'the Comedy of Menace'.
Dramatic suspense is derived both from the characters' fear
and from the ambiguity about whether they really need to be
afraid.

The scene between Stella and Charles introduces past history far
more skilfully than this was done in *Conditions of Agreement*, with a
good deal of underlying tension and using the dinner in London very
cleverly to skirt round the danger of writing a conversation in which
(for the sake of the audience) husband and wife tell each other what they
both know already. We soon gather that Stella has followed her father
into exile and that his relations with the village are symptomatic of

15

his relations with society as a whole. Charles is another artist who has cut himself off from society and, not wanting an audience for himself, he doesn't share Stella's wish to rehabilitate Paul as a great writer.

Breach of contact with society is also thematic in *Marching Song* and *The Gates of Summer*. The protagonists of *A Penny for a Song*, though not exiles or prisoners, are comically cut off from the realities (social, political, military) and *The Devils* is about a hero martyred by a community which unites against him.

The tension in *Saint's Day* is tightened still further when it becomes obvious that Stella is not coming out into the open about her reasons for wanting to re-establish Paul in society. When she suggests that Charles should be introduced to Robert as her younger brother, we are mystified by her motives. After the vague menace and the unfulfilled threats of *Conditions of Agreement*, Whiting has learned to use mystification as a means of focusing our attention precisely where he needs it. We become very curious about what's going to happen.

Paul's entrance is another dramatic one. We hear him talking to John Winter as they come down the stairs and their conversation grows more audible as the tension between Charles and Stella snaps into an unpleasant little quarrel when he finds a white hair in her head and Paul comes in before Charles has answered her question, 'I'm ugly to you, aren't I?' Having two conversations going at the same time adds to the impression that a great deal is happening fast and the same device is used again when Stella and Charles start whispering together inaudibly while Paul talks to John Winter and again, most noticeably of all, when Stella is talking to John Winter about the shopping he's brought back from the village while Paul talks to Charles about Robert's non-appearance.

There's an oddly tense moment when Paul unwraps the scarf Charles has knitted for his birthday present saying, 'I hope it isn't green. I don't like green things.' It is green. This would have been effective whatever colour Whiting had chosen but green has an association with spring and Nature and youth and fertility, so Paul's hatred of it may combine with his intention of cutting down the trees, his age and the frequent mention of John

Winter's surname to start some of the audience thinking in seasonal terms.*

As Paul describes the trees, 'blanched by age – withered, contorted, and monstrous', they become identified with him and the urgency of his wish to cut them down becomes suggestive of his self-destructiveness. At the end of Act Two he tears the scarf from his neck at the climax of his 'terrible paroxysm of grief and fear'. He wants to 'do himself great physical violence, but his strength fails him'.

As in *Waiting for Godot*, which was written the same year, much of the dialogue consists of very short lines indeed, which makes it sound more colloquial than it is, and the occasional literary speech, like Stella's about the trees, stands out in clear relief.

> They were most benevolent to Ellen and me when we were children. They were almost our only playthings and gave themselves so willingly to masquerading as other places – other worlds.

Paul's lines give hints of identifying him with the dog, as well as with the trees.

> STELLA: He's so large and he will come into the house – and he's begun to smell terribly.
> PAUL: Probably I do. I'm getting old. I suppose I shan't be allowed in the house soon.
> STELLA: Don't pity yourself.
> PAUL: What did you say?
> STELLA: Nothing.

This is typical – abrupt thrusts which cut through to the attitude behind the lines and then a quick change of subject to parry the threat that the insight provokes. Eliot tends to freeze his characters into a temporary choric function at moments of insight. Whiting does this in the 'point of deviation' speech, but makes much more use of the thrust and parry technique.

* It is even possible that the scarf is a reference to the green girdle in *Sir Gawain and the Green Knight*, a fourteenth-century poem in which Gawain beheads the Knight on New Year's Day. The trunk picks up the head and rides off ordering the hero to meet him again a year hence. The girdle which he's given is meant to make him invulnerable, and it may be significant that Paul leaves the scarf behind when he goes out to his death. The child picks it up.

John Whiting

Paul is obviously the saint of the title though Robert also undergoes a conversion. It's Paul's birthday on the day of the action, January 25th, the accepted anniversary of the conversion of St Paul. While Robert loses his faith in Man, Paul, at least to some extent, regains his. The word saintliness rather surprisingly occurs in another rhetorical speech when Stella tries to comfort Paul.

> You are greater than any of them. They understand that by these last twenty-five years of exile and mortification you have proved the justice and truth of those opinions expressed in your pamphlets. You have proved your integrity and saintliness and tonight it is that that they will honour. Paul! You're not going before a tribunal.

And there's another hint of saintliness when he blesses the soldiers, and though he's hardly a saint in fact, he's not an ordinary man either. As in *Marching Song*, the word 'man' recurs a lot, particularly when the dialogue dwells on the lowest common multiples of humanity. Whiting is always interested in heroes who rise above their fellow men in one way or another, and, except in *Conditions of Agreement* the reasons for the exile or imprisonment are connected with the features that distinguish the heroes from the rest. But Paul is old and frail and frightened and Stella has to comfort him in her most rhythmic speech yet.

> Joking or not – that is what you must do. Play the great man. Now, at this moment, you may tell me of your fears. At this moment, because we are alone and I love you. But from the time of Procathren's coming here you must act the great man. You must meet this elegant and witty young man with your own elegance and wit. Good gracious me! From what Mamma told me you were a great one for acting in your day. (PAUL *laughs*.) Were you? Then remember that when you meet these people.

She is feminine but firm. As in some of Catherine's attempts to reassure Rupert, the soft, lulling cadences in the rhetoric serve a dramatic purpose. But the staccato phrases like 'Good gracious me!' and 'Were you?' interrupt and alter the rhythm.

Charles and Paul are amused over the cutting from an old *Tatler* which shows Robert photographed after his wedding to Miss Amanda

18

Mantis, daughter of Mr and Mrs Sebastian Mantis, and this produces a scene which is almost like a revue sketch. They're joining satirical forces against Stella, as later they will against Robert.

> PAUL: Look! Look, Charles, what do they say?
> CHARLES: '– distinguished young poet and critic —'
> PAUL: '– distinguished young poet and critic —'
> CHARLES (*he nudges* PAUL): Paul, my old one —
> PAUL (*giggling with anticipation*): Yes? Yes, sonny, yes?
> CHARLES: A splendid young man. Isn't he, Stella? Paul – Paul, tell me —
> PAUL: Yes, sonny? Yes, what?
> CHARLES: Isn't he the kind of young man Stella admires – very much admires? Clean, upright, bold —
> PAUL: Yes? Yes?
> CHARLES: – full of a passionate desire – for life. Not like us, my ancient – not like you and me – being, as we are, despised by Stella. No, she'd admire him – this Procathren.

Stella doesn't hit back until John Winter returns with the food. He reports in a military style on the situation in the village and Paul behaves like a Commander-in-Chief. Stella's satire punctures his inflated military grandeur and he's at once reduced to the stature of a pathetic old man. Whiting has a keen eye for the effect people have on each other when they release their latent hostility, and Paul's age makes him vulnerable.

> All right, Captain Winter. Take General Southman to his room.
> PAUL: Stella – I —
> STELLA: Go along, Grandpa. You can hatch your revolutionary schemes as well up there as you can down here.
> (JOHN WINTER *takes* PAUL'S *arm and they begin to move to the stairs.*)
> PAUL: Where's that copy of Alice, Charles?
> CHARLES: I'll bring it to you.
> STELLA: You're not to read. You're to rest.
> PAUL: Charles said I could read.
> STELLA: No, you're to rest.

Left alone with Charles, Stella has an extremely long speech (two

19

and a half pages of script) much of it literary in style but with colloquial interruptions of her own rhythm. She talks about 'this tortured family' and 'this damned house' almost as if it were cursed, like the house of Atreus. She stresses the fact that she's a woman.

> Try to remember, Charles, that I am a woman – try to be conscious of that at other times than when I am naked. I am a woman and I have a child inside me. Does that explain anything to you? Pregnant women have delusions, they say. Do they? I know nothing about it. Am I deluded, Charles? Am I? I only know that I am possessed by a loneliness hard to bear – a loneliness which I should imagine attends forsaken lovers. (*She stands silent – then*) Lovers. I am innocent of such things. I have imagined what they do and what they say – these lovers. It seems they find a great delight in music and solicitude, in whispering and smiling, in touching and nakedness, in night. And from these things they make a fabric of memory which will serve them well in their life after death when they will be together but alone. They are wise, for that is the purpose of any memory – of any experience – to give foundation to the state of death. Understand that whatever we do today in this house – this damned house – will provide some of the material for our existence in death and you understand my fear. No one who has lived as I have lived could be happy in death. It is impossible. Why don't you speak? Now! Why don't you speak, now? You could have released me – you could have freed me from this place if only you could have overcome your fear of the world out there and returned yourself. Even now you could kill my black, desperate, damnable fear of all time being empty if you would tell me – show me how to love. I am human and I am a woman. Tell me. And, O, Charles, Charles, comfort me!

This can be very moving in the theatre but at the Stratford East revival it was badly staged, with Stella sitting at a table and Charles circling round it away from her. He should be static, trying to turn away from the force of what she says. She is the one who needs to be moving, trying to break in on his self-containment. The speech is intensely but justifiably rhetorical, saying a good deal that couldn't be said in colloquial language. The lilt of the sentences about lovers helps to show that she is not talking from experience, and the idea

she introduces of building up memories as a foundation for the
state of death is important to the play. Robert returns to it in his big
speech at the end and it adds to the momentousness of what we see
happening. What foundation are these people laying for their
deaths?

The answer to her plea for comfort is a blast on a trumpet. Neither
of them know what it is, but it's obviously a threat of some sort from
the outside world.

Whiting finds any number of ways of giving a theatrical perspective on time and there's a good example at the beginning of Act
Two when Paul, convinced that Robert isn't coming, says, 'It isn't so
long ago since I could see that clock from here' – a sentence which
pinpoints both the minute-to-minute progression of time within
the play's action and the gradual deterioration of Paul's eyesight over
the last few months.

Robert's belated arrival is highly dramatic. None of them see
him as he comes in and he stands silently in the doorway till Paul
reaches the end of his brilliant speech about society, a speech which
helps us to believe in him as a great satirist by giving some hint of
what his pamphleteering style might have been like.

> The accusation against Paul Frederick Southman! (*He beats on
> the arm of his chair.*) 'Paul Frederick Southman: you are charged
> with the assault of the well-known and much-beloved whore,
> Society, in that you did, with malice and humour, reveal her for
> what she is and not for what men wish her to be, thereby
> destroying the illusion of youth and the wisdom of age. Also
> that you employed the perversion of using for this purpose your
> pen instead of the recognized organ.' Witnesses called for the
> prosecution. Andrew Vince: this witness testified the poor old
> body to be sadly shaken by her experience and vehemently
> denied the defence's suggestion that he had rummaged her
> after finding her crying in an alley. John Ussleigh: this witness,
> a publisher, stated that he saw the assault but had been under
> the impression that it was a case of true love. He had known the
> prisoner for a number of years, etc. etc. An unnamed young
> man: this witness, called for medical evidence, admitted inter-
> course with Society on several occasions. When asked by the
> defence whether he was not repelled by the malformations of

21

John Whiting

Society, he answered, 'I thought all women were like that.' Witnesses called for the defence: none. Sentence: exile.

Robert's opening clichés seem particularly colourless by contrast. This is the rhetoric of self-conscious pomposity.

> Surely, Mr Southman, there is no necessity for formality between us on this occasion but there are a few things I should like to say. Have I your permission?
> (PAUL *is silent.*)
> STELLA: Please go on.
> ROBERT: Thank you. I'll be brief. (*He speaks to* PAUL.) What I am doing in coming here today —
> PAUL: Did John Winter say he'd feed the dog?
> STELLA: Yes, Grandpa. (*To* ROBERT) You must forgive him.
> ROBERT: Of course. I appreciate the honour you do me in allowing me to come here, to this house, today – this house which has been closed to the world for so many years.

Whiting exploits the dog in several surprising and effective ways. Later, when Robert is puzzled at being asked whether it annoyed him, he says that it's dead and Paul rushes out of the room to investigate, returning with the pistol in his hand, convinced that the villagers have poisoned it and that reprisals are called for.

It's during the absence of Paul and Charles that Stella makes her strange appeal to Robert:

> STELLA: You are young, you are famous and powerful, you are talented and you can do as I ask.
> ROBERT (*he laughs*): I am a minor poet – nothing more.
> STELLA: Why do you laugh?
> ROBERT: I don't know.
> STELLA: At this moment – why do you laugh?
> ROBERT: Shyness, I suppose. I am shy.
> STELLA: I'm sorry but there's no time for the courtesies and formalities as between strangers. You mustn't expect them from me. But please don't withdraw. A moment ago you were willing to help me.
> ROBERT: I don't understand what you want.
> STELLA: This! This is what I want! I want Paul to be restored to his former greatness. In that way there can be a future for my child.

ROBERT: Your child?
STELLA: I'm pregnant. The child Paul. Innocent, you will admit – in no way responsible. For the child's sake old Paul must be restored to greatness in the world.

As with Nicholas's and Peter's hostility to A.G., it's difficult to believe in the motives that the character gives and it's not altogether clear whether Whiting wants us to, but in any case the appeal works as a kind of litmus test on Robert, who emerges very badly from it. The satire on him is extremely funny and we feel that if this man is representative of the literary world, we sympathize with Paul's rejection of it. Paul's opinion of Robert is obviously never high but it sinks lower when he says that he doesn't want to be involved in the affair with the villagers. But he lets himself be persuaded and it's here, feeling she's being betrayed, that Stella comes out with her Eliot-like 'point of deviation' speech.

When Paul grills and ridicules Reverend Aldus, and when Charles joins in the fun Paul has over Robert's inexperience with firearms, both exiles are showing their contempt for representatives of the Establishment. Aldus is all the more pathetic because of his stammer and after he's gone Paul calls him a circus clown, while Robert, playing with the pistol, seems much less of a man than Paul or Charles. The baiting scene is a great advance on the baiting scene in *Conditions of Agreement* and still closer in spirit to *The Birthday Party* (written ten years later).

CHARLES: Surely you must have been engaged in some war —
ROBERT: No.
CHARLES: – at your age.
ROBERT: No. I was not fit.
CHARLES: Morally or physically?
ROBERT: Both.
CHARLES: You fought with your pen, eh?
PAUL: Have you never —
CHARLES: Poems of victory!
ROBERT: And defeat.
PAUL: Have you never been moved —
CHARLES: Bravo!
PAUL: – moved by hate or persecution —

O   23

CHARLES: Or love?
PAUL: – to contemplate physical violence?
ROBERT: Never.
CHARLES: It has always been unemotional, calm force —
PAUL: – in boxing rings —
CHARLES: – with rules —
PAUL: – and referees —
CHARLES: – against harmless little boys.

The tension that's wound up in this is given an immediate theatrical outlet when the pistol goes off in Robert's hand but we don't yet know that the bullet has travelled through the door and killed Stella or that in firing it Robert has 'lost his innocence'.

The discovery of Stella's body is extremely theatrical. Another blast on the trumpet outside may produce a premonition of catastrophe but Paul, failing to recognize it for what it is, opens the window to welcome the soldiers as allies, shouting a blessing to them. No answer comes from the soldiers but in the silence while the three men are waiting, another shout comes from the bottom of the stairs. It's John Winter. Robert realizes this is the call from another room, Charles notices Stella hasn't come back from seeing Aldus out and when he runs to the door, he can't open it. He has to throw his whole weight against it to shift the obstruction on the other side and in the ensuing confusion, while Charles rushes out shouting for help and John Winter helps to carry Stella's body in, Robert is silently digesting what's happened to him and Paul is withdrawing Lear-like into unreality.

Robert is alone in the room when the soldiers come. Killeen and Chater are much more like clown figures than Aldus and perform magnificent mock bows to Robert. The unnaturalistic alliance between him and the soldiers starts when he asks them not to go, and Melrose supports him when he seems about to fall. 'What have they made me do?' he asks. Just as Charles's support, whether silent or spoken, enabled Paul to insult Aldus and Robert, the support of the soldiers, who have already left, gives Robert the strength to insult Paul. 'Beast-face' he calls him. Robert is no longer the same man and though the change in him is hard for an audience to understand intellectually, the extraordinary events of the act and the extraordinary pressure behind Whiting's presentation of them make it acceptable theatrically.

It's only in Act Three that *Saint's Day* begins to lose its coherence and its force. So far nearly all the elements in the play have worked both realistically and symbolically; here the seams begin to come undone. The style of the writing shifts as the parody element gains too much of the upper hand and Whiting moves from T. S. Eliot to his Greek sources, with four village women and a child on-stage throughout as a makeshift chorus, and a long messenger narration from the village postman. Mystification, skilfully controlled as an appetizer in Act One, sticks in our throats at this stage of the meal, especially as so much of the main action is now off-stage and we have to make do with second-hand accounts of it. It's not at first clear why the women are here, who started the fire in the village or where our attention ought to be focused. The characters who have held our interest suddenly aren't there. Stella's dead, Paul has withdrawn into madness, Charles is now too much of a foil and Robert, who is the main protagonist in this act, having taken over the initiative, doesn't appear until almost the end of the play.

Several elements make a strong impact – the sky reddened by the fire, Stella's corpse which Charles is using as a model to finish his painting, the noise of bells ringing, the bones on the floor at the foot of the bier, the child bouncing a ball and the women themselves, filling one side of the stage. Sitting in the firelight surrounded by odd articles salvaged from their houses and nondescript bundles of belongings, they also serve as a reminder of the refugee situation in Europe as it still was in 1951. But while Whiting certainly succeeds in conveying the impression that things of major importance are happening, he doesn't this time feed us the right flow of information in the right way to satisfy the appetite he's whetted. The killing which comes at the end of the act is still moving but not as moving as it might have been if the build-up to it had been better.

The village postman, Cowper, is an amusing figure with his bucolic self-righteousness and his pride in taking over the duties of P.C. Pogson. It's unrealistic that he should be sent to ask the people at the house to make statements about the fire but this is the half-hearted pretext for the dialogue which leads up to his long narrative. This contains a lot of essential information about what's happening in the village and it's amusing as parody, but it might have been better to present it without trying to graft it semi-realistically into the action. As it is, it's too patently a stratagem to cover the structural weakness caused by shifting the main action to the village, where the soldiers are now acting under Robert's destructive orders.

Blooded, like an animal, by his experience of killing, Robert is taking a terrible revenge against the social order with which he'd always been such an ardent conformist. Instead of bringing Paul back to society, he's himself turning against it. But none of this can possibly become clear from Cowper's description of how the big soldier had his arm around the dandy fellow and how the dandy fellow was talking and talking and how Aldus, crying like a baby, was pulling the valuable books off his shelves to throw on the fire. Aldus, as we find out later when Melrose tells Charles, had been listening to Robert, who destroyed his belief in the old order of things.

Paul, on the other hand, is converted to a surprising friendliness towards the villagers. When he finds the women installed in his living-room he welcomes them and he spends most of his time talking to the child. But when Charles, realistically facing up to the fact of their imminent destruction, says 'I shall work till the last minute,' Paul is unwilling or unable to come to grips with the reality. After playing at soldiering, he can't face the truth about what the soldiers stand for. He still seems to believe that Robert's going to drive him to London and he talks about chopping down the trees while he's waiting. Charles has his most literary speech in telling him off:

> CHARLES: Damn you, Paul! God damn you for the beastliness – the selfishness of shutting yourself up in your tower of senility and lunacy at this moment – at this moment!
>
> PAUL: Hush, Charles! You'll frighten the child.
>
> CHARLES: If only I could take refuge in madness as you have done. If only I could convince myself, as you have done, that I am an artist, that the world waited to honour me, that the fires out there were a display for a victory, that these brushes I hold were sceptres and these people princes. Then I might face the future! You have the belief and the refuge – but it is not for me. I cannot go so far. I am not mad. I am not mad.

> God help me! I can touch the reality and know that I am nothing, that the world censures me, that the fires burn without reason, that these brushes are instruments of torture and these people miserable, frightened clods!

The charge of beastliness is an echo of Robert's 'Beast-face' and the grouping of the characters according to whether or not they can 'touch the reality' is to be repeated in *Marching Song*, where Rupert and Dido are the realists, Catherine and Harry the romantics.

Paul ignores the rebuke and rambles on to the child, confusing her with his dead grand-daughter, though he doesn't know that she too is called Stella. (Stella's unborn baby was going to be called Paul.) The little girl, like the boy in *A Penny for a Song* and the boy in *No Why*, never answers anything the adults say to her – except to say 'Many happy returns of the day' and when Paul describes the reception in London, Whiting cleverly makes his words ambiguous. He could equally well be referring to his reception in Heaven.

> 'Many happy returns of the day,' you said. And that is what they will say when I arrive – the great and famous people receiving me – they will say — *And the little crowd, speaking together, say,* 'Many happy returns of the day' – *and then, possessed by quite a tiny fever of excitement, they cry out separately,* 'Happy birthday' – 'God bless you' – 'Much happiness to you' *and* 'Good men are rewarded'.

The chorus is giving him the accolade Dido gives Rupert when she says, 'You seem to me a very good man.' This is Whiting's basic concern – what it is to be a man and what it is to be a good one. The little dance Paul does for the child, which cues the soldiers' entrance, is a link to the dance that the child performs at the end of the play when Paul is killed, having demurred at dancing for him now. His belief that he's still going to London gives his dialogue with Melrose a double meaning:

PAUL: Have you come for me?
MELROSE: That's right.
PAUL: I'm ready. Look, I'm quite ready.
MELROSE: Were you expecting me?
PAUL: Oh yes. (*To the* CHILD) No more dancing now.

John Whiting

For us, sensing but not knowing that he's going to die, these lines have the ring of doom about them.

As Melrose speaks to Charles and as Chater silently makes nooses out of the ropes John Winter has brought for cutting down the trees, Paul's dialogue with the child works as a chilly counterpoint. His spectacle case becomes a crocodile snapping at the child's nose.

> And it comes along – along – along – and snap!

All this is intensely effective. The false note comes when Whiting tries to explain why the soldiers are going to kill Charles and the old man:

> Bobby doesn't think I'm capable. He's dared me to do it. (*He stands up, smiling.*) That's a silly thing to do, isn't it? What does he think I am? What does he think I shall feel? You're nothing to me – neither's the old man. Nobody's anything to me – because there is nobody – hasn't been for years. I care for nothing. They put it right when they said I was an 'incorrigible'.

This would have been better left unsaid, and it's equally over-explicit when Melrose gives Charles his diagnosis of what Paul and he have done to Robert.

> You've brought this on yourselves. People like us shouldn't do such things to people like that – people who live away out there with women and music. You've struck him very deep. He's talked to me about it and my God! can't he talk. He told me about it, all right. I didn't understand one word in ten about his guilt and the way you've destroyed his innocence – but I understood a little. Poor Bobby!

Three-quarters of the act is over before Robert appears, his clothes torn and filthy, his face blackened by the fire. He's been sick and Killeen has to wipe him down. Melrose's insistence that Robert takes the responsibility for what's happening makes us think of the refrain of the German war criminals and the excuse for so many wartime atrocities: I was acting under orders.

> If you want to order people like me around you've got to take the responsibility – you've got to. It's always been like that. God knows, I wouldn't have it any other way. But it makes me

28

laugh sometimes. 'Melrose do such-and-such!' 'Yes, sir!' – and then I look down and see their eyes and their eyes are asking me, 'Melrose you think that decision is right, don't you? If you think I'm wrong for God's sake don't do it.' But I do it whatever I think – if I can be bothered to think. What is it I can do for you, Bobby?

The elements which should have been explicated in the action of this act are all concertina'd into one long, difficult speech, full of conceits:

ROBERT: Southman – I thought the power invested was for good. I believed we were here to do well by each other. It isn't so. We are here – all of us – to die. Nothing more than that. We live for that alone. You've known all along, haven't you? Why didn't you tell me – why did you have to teach me in such a dreadful way? For now – (*he cries out*) – I have wasted my inheritance! All these years trying to learn how to live leaving myself such a little time to learn how to die. (*He turns to speak to the* CHILD) Afraid of the dark? But it is more than the dark. It is that which lies beyond, not within, the dark – the fear of the revelation by light. We are told by our fairy-tale books that we should not fear but the darkness is around us, and our fear is that the unknown hand is already at the switch. I tell you, do not fear, for there is no light and the way is from darkness to darkness. (PAUL *takes* ROBERT'S *hand and holds fast to it.* ROBERT *again speaks to him.*) You old rascal! Knowing it is not a question of finding but of losing the pieties, the allegiances, the loves. You should tell. I've been talking to Aldus. Told him I lost faith in God years ago and never felt its passing. But man – oh, take faith in man from me and the meaning becomes clear by the agony we suffer. What a cost it is. Clear – not for all immediately – no, Aldus is out there at the moment chasing his lost God like a rat down a culvert. But for myself – I am well. (*He moves from* PAUL.) Perhaps I should have understood before coming here. There are many signs out in the world offering themselves for man's comprehension. The flowers in the sky, the sound of their blossoming too acute for our ears leaving us to hear nothing but the clamour of voices protesting, crying out against the end – 'It's not fair!' – as they fasten to the walls of

> life – and the storm of their own making – it is the howling
> appeal for tenderness, for love. Only now I see the thing's
> played out and compassion – arid as an hour-glass – run
> through. Such matters need not concern us here in this – (*for
> a moment he is silent*) – in this place. For we have our own
> flowers to give us understanding. (*He points to* STELLA.) The
> rose she wears beneath her heart. There, released, is the
> flower within us all – the bloom that will leap from the breast
> or drop from the mouth. It shall be my conceit that a flower
> is our last passport. Who wears it shall go free. Free, South-
> man!

This has some beautiful and arresting phrases in it but in its theatrical context it doesn't work so well as Stella's best speeches. It's much harder for an audience to follow and it's too obviously put in as an attempt at a rational explanation of the irrational changes in Robert. He oversimplifies in a way Stella didn't: she never made bald statements like 'We're here – all of us – to die.' To say that the purpose of life is to build a foundation for death is, in a way, enhancing life because it makes it all the more important to use the time to create the right fabric of memories. If Robert has failed to do this, it's not because of any lack of knowledge but because, like Stella's, his life has been empty of love. The beginning of the speech sounds far too explicit and it's a very awkward bridge to the Eliot-like lines about the fear of the revelation by light (which may also be an allusion to the conversion of St Paul) and the unknown hand already at the switch. All through the speech the tone is uncertainly dogmatic. Stella spoke out of emotions she was currently feeling; Robert seems to have spent all his passion in off-stage action. If Robert didn't try to explain things, we'd accept anything, but any attempt at explanation is bound to draw attention to how much is being left unexplained. Why has his involvement in Stella's accidental death taken away his faith in man? What he is saying to the child is that there's no reason to be afraid of anything because there's nothing beyond the darkness except more darkness. People may well be wrong to fear punishment but nothing that's happened in the action justifies his assertion that it's always wrong to expect tenderness or love from other people, whether or not they've learnt the painful lesson he's learnt. Paul and Charles were obviously teasing him but now he's punishing them for choosing not to teach him the same lesson in a more gentle way and, madly, he's blaming them because he didn't learn long ago, long before he met them. But his madness isn't in focus and it's not at all clear how far Whiting is wanting to stand back from him at this point. The imagery which links the flower with blood and death isn't very well worked out and altogether the speech leaves us feeling it would have made more sense if it hadn't tried to make so much.

Though it detracts from the effectiveness of the killing, the ending still makes a very strong impact. Paul goes out to his death believing that the soldiers and Robert are bringing the ropes to help him cut down the trees. Melrose gives some money to John Winter who immediately calls him sir. The stage is left to the villagers. It's when the child touches Stella's dead face that we hear her name for the first time. 'Stella,' the mother calls. It's as if she were the New Year taking over the identity of the dead year. She picks up the green scarf and, putting it round her neck, she performs a grave dance to the raucous little tune the trumpet plays. It's not the dead being raised but the living raised to death. When the sound stops, she runs to her mother and buries her head in the woman's lap.

A PENNY FOR A SONG

For a play written so soon after *Saint's Day*, *A Penny for a Song* is an astonishing contrast, satirical but inoffensive, sharp but happy, an amused celebration of English vagueness and the delights of a summer day in the country. In 1949, when Whiting wrote it, Arthur Koestler was still fulminating against our English deafness to the Cassandra cries of political prophets (like himself) and our blindness towards political realities. Whiting, less angry but no less sceptical, made Koestler's point in one quiet, beautiful, funny piece of stage action. In the middle of the Napoleonic invasion scare, with a poster proclaiming 'Invasion' stuck to a tree, the Bellboys family settle down to a picnic tea on the lawn. A loud explosion is heard and a cannon-ball rolls into the garden. They ignore it. A second explosion and a second cannon-ball bounds in, to come to rest next to the first.

> HESTER: Lamprett!
> LAMPRETT: My dear?
> HESTER: Shut the gate.

An unpublished Ph.D. thesis, *A Private Mythology. The Development of the Dramatic Art of John Whiting and a Comparative Study of his Major Plays*, by Gabrielle Scott Robinson quotes from an article of Whiting's published in a May 1952 issue of *The Bath Critic* in which he says that the idea for the play occurred to him on seeing an English garden in 1940 during the invasion scare. It was a very happy inspiration to use history as a comic alienation effect, treating a similar but much more distant scare with one eye cocked humorously on the eternal problem of what the private individual can do under the shadow of current political realities when he has no faith that the authorities are taking the right actions. And part of the joke of *A Penny for a Song* is that none of the eccentric reactions of the characters are invented by Whiting. As he says in his introduction to *The Plays of John Whiting*, 'It is rarely necessary to embroider the finer lunacies of the English at war.' Mrs Robinson, who had access

to a number of Whiting's private papers, found a manuscript titled
'*Notes for a Comedy* July 1948' in which Whiting took notes from
Carola Oman's book *Britain Against Napoleon*. This was obviously
a main source for the play and it shows how many of his ideas were
founded on fact. Rich landowners really did recruit their own corps,
training them at their own expense. There were 'Fencibles' like the
St Pancras and Marylebone Volunteers and even the price of the
invasion posters is historically correct. The paragraph Mrs Robinson
quotes from Carola Oman's book gives the germ of several themes in
the play.

> A thrilling, but not well attested rumour, declared that he had
> under construction a monster bridge, by which his troops were
> to pass from Calais to Dover, directed by skilled officers in air
> balloons, and a Channel Tunnel, engineered by a mining expert.
> The most dramatic tale was that the Emperor, disguised as a
> British tar, was aboard a south coast fishing smack. He patrolled
> England's shores by night, and during the hours of daylight
> spied ashore.

Like *Conditions of Agreement, Saint's Day* and *Marching Song, A
Penny for a Song* observes the Aristotelian unities but it weaves many
more characters and more strands of action into the one day. (In
Marching Song it's just over thirty-six hours.) Just as *Saint's Day*
differentiates between Paul's fantasy of waging war against the
villagers and the actuality of the violence when it comes, *A Penny
for a Song* differentiates between the two characters who have actually
had experience of war and the others who live out their fantasies of
defensive action against the French. Sir Timothy's idea of dressing
up as Napoleon, polishing up his French from a phrase book, crawling
through a tunnel to come out behind the invading army and ordering
it to retreat would take the booby prize for misplaced ingenuity in
any village competition, but it's scarcely wilder than the rumour of
Napoleon dressed as a British sailor, from which it may derive.

The others are all endearingly useless in much the same way –
Lamprett, with his obsessive firefighting, which makes him vie with
Sir Timothy for the services of the unfortunate Humpage, who has
been posted in the tree as a look-out; Hester, with her eagerness to

go up to East Anglia to command a platoon in Lady Jerningham's Amazon Corps and George Selincourt, with his breezy naïvety in commanding the local Fencibles.

For the revival of the play at the Aldwych in August 1962, Whiting did a lot of rewriting, changing the play a good deal – on the whole, unfortunately for the worse. Perhaps he then found the play which Peter Brook had directed in 1951 at the Haymarket too 'charming'. The chief object of the changes seems to have been to prune away all indulgence in 'charm' and all generalized philosophizing.

In the original script, Edward Sterne is blind. That he's a victim of the war is the most obvious thing about him and he's dependent on Jonathan, using him as a kind of visual antenna. The little boy never speaks but nods and shakes his head and whispers in Edward's ear, and he's guiding Edward to London where he wants to see the King and get him to stop the war. He's convinced that he'll achieve this just by showing himself to him. Jonathan is then bound for Bethlehem, believing himself to be the brother of Jesus and not knowing that it's 1800 years since Jesus was born. In the later version Edward has his sight and also has a very large chip on the shoulder. He's militantly radical and obstreperously didactic.

> EDWARD: Look, Dorcas, the world's full of people. Yes?
> DORCAS: I suppose so.
> EDWARD: Believe me, it is. And they live in many different states of power and weakness, wealth and poverty. Right?
> DORCAS: Er, yes.
> EDWARD: There was a revolution in France, and there's been one in America.
> DORCAS: Yes, it was very shocking.
> EDWARD: You are a silly girl! It wasn't shocking, it was perfectly splendid. Now, say after me: Revolution is a good thing.

Quiet jokes like having Hallam read Wordsworth as an example of radical thinking are swept away in the flood of Edward's noisy radicalism. Altogether he upsets the filigree equilibrium of the play by his heavy-handed Left Wing rightmindedness. The original Edward is just as wrong-headed as everyone else in the play and when Hallam warns him gently that he won't do any good by seeing the

King, who is mad, it provides a beautiful deflation, rather like the ironic deflations in *The Gates of Summer*. The second Edward is so aggressively, sanely practical that he becomes an unnecessary yardstick for measuring the eccentricity of the other characters. He doesn't belong to the same world as the Bellboys family, and by letting him argue against them, Whiting loses a lot of the play's tender subtlety.

As in *Saint's Day*, the action gets going very quickly. Several well-varied characters are established briskly and they talk in clean-cut, abrupt sentences which make them seem clean-cut and rather abrupt in themselves. It's pleasant to have conversations carried on high above stage level as people throw open first-floor windows to speak to Humpage in the tree and Whiting soon gets things going with criss-cross conversations. Sir Timothy argues with Humpage about which way the wind's blowing while Hester asks her daughter Dorcas how old she is and, hearing she's seventeen, tells her to put off childish ways. We gather that as in *Conditions of Agreement*, the transition from childhood to adult life is going to be one of the themes, but it's not going to be treated straightforwardly. The grown-ups are in many ways more childish than Dorcas or Jonathan who, particularly in the 1962 version, has had experience of the war.

> He was conceived, born and brought up for the first six years of his life in a wagon. Then at 'Linden his father was killed, and his mother ran off with a quartermaster. Peace was signed and we were all told to go home. But his home was upturned in a ditch. So we started walking.

In this version it's Edward who's helped Jonathan; in 1951 Edward had been in Jonathan's debt ever since he felt Jonathan's warm hand taking hold of his.

As in *Saint's Day* and *Marching Song*, the characters often look at themselves from outside.

HESTER: Do I bully you?
LAMPRETT (*he smiles*): A little.
HESTER (*she smiles*): Forgive me. I must a little or belie my appearance.

John Whiting

But not all the characters can be as self-conscious as this or it would interfere with the comedy of their obsessiveness. Lamprett's only interest in the prospect of invasion is in the fires that will get started during the battle. They will make life difficult for him.

> For while we must extinguish our own fires we must be careful to foster those of the enemy.

Hallam, the philosophical visitor from London could easily have become a tedious *raisonneur* but he's as pleasingly eccentric as the others and in the 1951 version he makes a lot of funny and very affecting statements which disappear in 1962. He's amusingly self-conscious about his literariness and literary about his self-consciousness. After telling Hester that he wants peace, but not complete indifference to his welfare, he adds placatingly:

> There was a touch of asperity in that remark, wasn't there? Please forget it.

A Penny for a Song is a play without an exile or an ex-prisoner but Hallam is a temporary refugee from London.

> HESTER: How is London?
> HALLAM: London, my dear, is hell. I am in disgrace again. Like most men of my age I am in flight, pursued by the agony of love, the danger of war and the misery of democracy.

In 1951 his answer to her question is simply:

> In uproar. This invitation was God-sent.

Many different kinds of comedy – physical, situation, and verbal – are mixed in *A Penny for a Song* and not only are the joins neat but the moments are well judged when one kind takes over from another. There's an example of this after Timothy's entertaining but lengthy story, rather in the style of Laurence Sterne, of how Lamprett's obsession with fires started. Convinced that women should be admitted to Oxford colleges, he persuaded Hester to attend lectures for three weeks dressed in her uncle's second best ceremonial breeches. Smoking a pipe in front of the fire one evening she set light to them and after extinguishing the fire manually, Lamprett felt bound to marry her, and devoted his subsequent life to fighting fires. Telling

Hallam the story, Lamprett realizes that Humpage has been listening and orders him not to. Once Humpage has covered his ears with his hands, he's deaf to all Timothy's subsequent orders and it's only when Timothy arrives at the idea of throwing his hat in the air that he manages to make himself heard as Humpage's hands go out to catch it.

The scene when Timothy explains his plan to Hallam survives more or less unaltered and it's a good touch to make Timothy the originator of the Fencibles so that his madcap scheme of impersonation is his last resort when, against his will, an officer arrives from Taunton to take over command of his forces. But in the 1951 version there's a delightful moment at the end of the conversation when Hallam can hardly speak. He's convulsed with laughter and mistaking it for deep emotion at his braveness, Timothy is deeply moved himself. In the 1962 version this is cut.

The first scene between Hallam and the lovers is much less lyrical in the second version. Perhaps Whiting felt he was exposing too many of the nerves of his comedy when he had Hallam talking about the 'days when the clowns must sit together in the sun and talk of clownish things' and perhaps he later found Edward's answer to Dorcas's question 'Why do men fight each other?' too facile.

> Perhaps because there is a long-wished-for home they seek, and they are too frail to take upon themselves the responsibility for the journey. Did you never, when you were a baby, know of something you desired but of which – oh, so humanly – you were ashamed? And did you not, perhaps – shall we say – engineer that thing to come about – oh, so sinfully – through the fault of another? (*He smiles.*) You see, my life-loving darling, the dark journey to the dark home is sometimes sweeter than the summer's day.

But the new Edward is a bull in the china world of the Bellboys and I find his new political and social dogmatizing much more tiresome and no less over-explicit. Lines like this one, *à propos* of Hallam, gain very little by being put in Dorcas's mouth:

> He's the kind you meant when you said their passing would be like the melting of snow to show the promise of spring beneath, isn't he?

John Whiting

And it's a pity to lose Hallam's reflections on middle age.

> Yes! Try then to reconcile the ambitions and pure designs of youth with the failures and confusions of middle-age: the morning, sweet as a nut, with the early evening, sad as a mustard pot: reconcile the loves of boyhood with the friendships and harsh passions of *nel mezzo del cammin di nostra vita*. (*He pauses.*) I think I'm going to cry.

This is a Fry-like passage but it fits in with the rest of the play much better than the new elements which seem to constitute an ineffective compromise gesture in the direction of the drama of social consciousness.

> For the last four years I've been walking about Europe. I've seen such horrible things that it broke my heart. Poverty and disease, love and friendship ruined by war, men and women living like animals in a desperate attempt to stay alive. I was one who sold himself for war so that he could eat, and I've had women sell themselves to me so that their children could eat. Now I may be simple, Matthews, but there's cause for all this. And the cause is laziness and indifference. There are only a handful of tyrants at any one time, but there are millions who don't care. I saw all this, I smelt it, I lay down with it at night, and at last I decided to fight. I carried in my pocket a book which is a weapon. It has a title which will mean nothing to you. It's called *The Rights of Man*.

The original *A Penny for a Song* was in no sense a play about European political realities: it was about an insular cloud-cuckooland, which was put perfectly in focus by the play.

In the 1951 version the first love scene is elegiac and delightful. Dorcas can't understand how Edward can love anything new, without seeing it. As always in Whiting, the woman makes the declaration of love to the man. The first Edward returns Dorcas's love; the second doesn't, which has a bad fomenting effect on her self-consciousness.

> DORCAS: After all, I'm still young enough to talk about a very common experience as if it were the most original thing in the world . . . Pooh, nobody understands how awful it is to be a

Marius Goring as Sir Timothy Bellboys in the revised version of *A Penny for a Song* at the Aldwych

Clive Morton (right), Marius Goring (centre, left) and Henry Woolf (centre) as George Selincourt, Sir Timothy Bellboys and Rufus Piggott in the revised version of *A Penny for a Song* at the Aldwych

child. All that loneliness and muddle. All that anger. Well, it's over now. Thank you very much. . . .

Judi Dench can get away with this outraged schoolgirl *saeva indignatio*, but Virginia McKenna had better, more serene lines to speak in 1951. Though one good touch in the new version is the very brief quarrel when Edward refuses not to go to London and Dorcas tells him to go now if he's going.

> EDWARD: What's this? A quarrel?
> DORCAS: Yes, it is. Good-bye. (*She stares into the distance.*)
> EDWARD: Good-bye.
> (*Neither of them move: silence.*)
> DORCAS: Forgive me.
> EDWARD: All forgotten.

In both versions there's a very nice build-up to the climax of activity which ends Act One. The sample Invasion poster which Selincourt has left on stage for Hallam alarms everyone else while Hallam sleeps peacefully on. Timothy rouses the dozing Humpage who catches sight of Selincourt's Fencibles and mistakes them for the enemy. He starts counting and the mounting figures are heard through the rest of the dialogue as they all rush around in a flurry of preparation. Lamprett primes Humpage. He tries to boost the morale of the silent Jonathan and, in the second version, Edward gives embittered instruction in the technique of survival.

> Don't stand under a flag, stay far away from anybody in a fine bright uniform, take a look at the sun so that you'll always know which way you're running, if there's a loaf of bread about put it in your pocket, and if there's a hole in the ground sit in it. Ignore all cries for help, stay deaf to all exhortations, and keep your trousers tied tight about your waist. In any difficulty, look stupid, and at the first opportunity go to sleep.

Breeze, Hallam's servant asks the advice of the others about whether to wake his master. Lamprett, standing by for reports of conflagrations, shakes hands gravely with Hallam, warning him not to tell the women what danger he's in, and he marches off with Jonathan. Timothy appears dressed as Napoleon and contradicts Humpage's

D

John Whiting

count of 116 with the assertion that there are a hundred and seventy-five men. Lamprett, called back by the sound of the bell which Timothy has ordered Humpage to sound, takes revenge for the misuse of his firebell by taking Timothy for Nelson. At the end of the act, about to go down the well with the bucket, Timothy stands in it letting Hallam take the full force of his weight while he speaks his heroic last words. Then when Hallam unwinds the rope nothing happens. Suddenly, after they're all distracted by the sight of the air-balloon, Timothy disappears with a loud cry, and with a final explosion the act is over.

The picnic scene which opens Act Two is extremely touching and funny. Lamprett and Hester realize that they haven't sat in the sun together for thirty years because there's always been too much to do. This makes, far more pleasantly, the point Dorcas makes in the 1962 version of her first scene with Edward when he says, 'I don't do anything just for pleasure' and she tells him, 'You should.' Mood and atmosphere build up beautifully and the cannon ball episode comes in the middle of a delicious piece of comedy as Lamprett self-importantly takes charge of the estate during Timothy's absence. He sounds like a parliamentary candidate making election promises.

> Under my direction things here will be very different. I've never agreed to the subordination of certain public services, such as the fire brigade, to ephemeral activities such as agriculture.

He has jumped to the conclusion that Timothy is trying to flee the country and when Hallam tries to tell him the facts, he won't listen.

The lovers are finally left alone with Hallam for a second trio, which is again very different from the corresponding scene in the first version. Hallam fusses over his meal and instead of smiling and answering 'No' as he did then in reply to the question of whether he was really so deeply concerned about himself, he now answers 'Certainly'. In the earlier version he told them that love was 'only a delicious pose to gain for ourselves the comfort we all so deeply need', and how even saints clown in the attempt to be other than they are. Edward's interpretation of Hallam's argument carried it forward:

> He means, I think, that we find the reality unbearable. That factor within us – ah! – the infrangible burden to carry: self-

40

knowledge. And so we escape, childlike, into the illusion. We clown and posture but not to amuse others – no – to comfort ourselves. The laughter is incidental to the tragic spectacle of each man attempting to hide his intolerable self.

And Hallam has a speech full of conceits linking Whiting's two favourite subjects, love and war:

We fight even our love from a catena of unprepared positions retiring ever deeper upon ourselves. The battle lost, we pretend the sacred citadel taken by the enemy is nothing more than a paper palace.

Admittedly there's no strong dramatic confrontation in all this but it's a pity to lose it and it's worse still to lose the scene in which Hallam takes Edward on one side to puncture his illusion about his audience with the King, encouraging him to go ahead and have it all the same.

In the revised version, all three characters are more bitter, less likeable. There's a good piece of reminiscence from Hallam about another summer's day fourteen years ago when he was in love and came to this garden, but it's all more desiccated than the original scene.

The words I both wrote and spoke came from my heart, and at the time were sincere, and not without beauty. Yet if they could be heard again in this garden we'd all be blushing. That is why old songs and dead fashion, which can make me cry, only make you laugh. That's what time can do. Cover my face.

The writing may be less wordy now, but there's less behind the words, less of a sense of suffering, and the scene is still conceived more in terms of monologue than of interaction. The nicest touch comes at the end when Hallam shows his understanding that Edward's less realistic outlook is more appealing.

Take her away, Sterne. She'll never be my sweetheart, but give me another half-hour with her and she'd be voting for me, if she could, in an election.

The very affecting scene between Hallam and Jonathan is also sacrificed:

John Whiting

What is it? Didn't they see you? (*The boy shakes his head.*)
Well, you're really very small, you know. Hasn't that got
anything to do with it? You're right, it hasn't. But you mustn't
be hurt: upset. Come here. (*The boy, unmoving, again shakes
his head.*) Now, why not? Do you think I'm going to talk to
you? To try to tell you why – why – why things happen. Do I
look like a great talker? I suppose I do: I am. But come here.
We'll sit together in absolute silence. Or do you like music to
pass the time? (HALLAM *takes from an inner pocket a tiny pipe
– a recorder – ludicrously small in comparison with his bulk. He
plays a snatch of a hornpipe. The child turns to him*) An unexpected accomplishment, eh? (*He continues to play and then holds
out the pipe to* JONATHAN) Try. (JONATHAN, *taking the pipe,
blows a single note.*) Were someone to overlook us now they would
take it that Innocence conversed with Experience. In that latter
part what can I say to you? I feel I should say something, don't
you? The situation requires it. Very well, then: retain the
defensive weapons of your childhood always, my dear. They are
invaluable, these delights and amusements. They are many,
too. And all so simple. Indeed, what is this? Only a wooden pipe
with some holes in it. But thrust a current of air through it –
there is a sound – and you smile and smile as you are smiling
now.

It's replaced by a passage which is safer, more guarded, but totally
lacking in magic. The chief joke in it is that Jonathan, who is now
French, after failing to react at all to anything Hallam has said,
suddenly laughs a lot when he quotes de la Rochefoucauld's line

On n'est jamais si heureux ni si malheureux qu'on s'imagine.

The next scene is rather like Shakespearean knockabout with the
well-meaning Selincourt drilling three of his Fencibles – a reverend
and two rustics. From Dogberry onwards, Shakespeare extracted a
lot of fun from the subject of inept civilians being bullied into an
unfamiliar discipline as soldiers or members of the Watch. And
Whiting, always fascinated by any form of soldiering, was quick to
see the comic possibilities of making non-soldiers ape the soldier.
After John Winter's military report on the situation in the village,
here we have the Rev. Brotherhood who, in making his report, introduces elements of the religious witch-hunt. His first reaction on seeing

Timothy was to start an exorcism. His second, taken in by the uniform and the French phrase, was to conclude it was Bonaparte.

The central strands in the comedy of misunderstandings now get woven closer together. Selincourt is happy in his conviction that Bonaparte has landed and he explains the absence of troops with the theory that the Emperor is bravely reconnoitring alone while his soldiers wait in a tunnel under the sea for the order to advance. And as Selincourt chases after Timothy, Lamprett rushes around putting out the fires he has lit to signal the start of the invasion. But before the pursuit sequences get going, a very literary joke is interposed. As the Fencibles go off, Rev. Brotherhood lags behind.

> BROTHERHOOD: Are you Hallam Matthews author of *A Critical Inquiry into the Nature of Ecclesiastical Cant*?
> HALLAM: 'With a Supplementary Dissertation on Lewd Lingo.' Yes, I am.
> BROTHERHOOD: You should be ashamed! (*Then he, too, is gone.*)

Then as Timothy floats blithely down in the gondola of a gaily painted balloon (Peter Brook's idea, according to Mrs Robinson), Hester takes his reappearance very much for granted: 'Oh, so you're back.' His physical position gives a big lift to his narrative of what's happened and the attempts of the others to get him down to earth provide a useful cross-current of action.

The *quid pro quo* is now developed from his side. He has mistaken the Fencibles for the French and the military exercise for the real thing. And again the comedy of action takes over from words when Timothy, trying desperately to get airborne again, orders Humpage to pull a cord which is dangling down from the balloon. It immediately starts to come down, neatly lowering Timothy into the well. As soon as he's disappeared, Selincourt comes back to announce that they're going to seal the mouth of the tunnel with explosives. After a trumpet blast and a countdown, there's a loud explosion and we're left in momentary suspense about whether Timothy's survived it.

Whiting follows the violent action with a quiet conversation. In the 1951 version, Hester tells the lovers something rather reminiscent of Stella's line about building a foundation for death.

John Whiting

People sometimes smile at the memory of your father and myself, but let me say this to you: remember the first day, my dears. It will mean much to you in the future.

These last two phrases are cut in 1962 but otherwise the scene is good, with pithy matter-of-fact statements about emotion reducing sentiment to a conversation-bubble minimum.

HESTER: You told us earlier – and we were a little sharp with you – that you are in love.
DORCAS: Yes, Mama.
HESTER: I can only presume it to be with this young man.
DORCAS: Yes.
HESTER: What did your father say?
DORCAS: That it was no time to be falling in love. When is a proper time, Mama?

When Selincourt and the Fencibles come on again, they cut in on each other's lines to describe how Timothy has been blown out of the mouth of the tunnel like a bullet from a gun. Both before and after the entrance of Jonathan and Lamprett, dirty from fire-fighting, tired and pleased with themselves, a good deal of riotous off-stage action is created through dialogue, all bubbling with good humour, all very much in the main tradition of the comedies that the English write about the English. Not only does Whiting distil a perfect English summer's day into stage action, he pokes gentle fun at our national blend of sportsmanship, pedantry, lunacy, pomposity, and propriety. Selincourt upbraids Lamprett for extinguishing the fires and Lamprett counters with the argument that once a fire's been started, it's public property. Selincourt rushes off in pursuit of Timothy, calling his Fencibles, like hounds, to follow and Timothy describes the experience of being blown up with a breezy devil-may-care condescension that beautifully parodies RAF wartime heroism.

Tried to blow me up, the devils. Inefficient fools! Ran some kind of mine which went off, and up I went like a rocket. Amazing sensation! Then, while they stood around gaping, I came to earth. Was rather stunned. Don't quite know what I did.

44

Timothy appears, of course, like Robert in *Saint's Day* and Harry in *Marching Song*, looking, ludicrous after the explosion and there's double comedy in the *quid pro quo* when, just to make sure that the real Bonaparte isn't here too, Hallam asks him whether he's seen anybody who looks like himself: he gets very indignant at the thought that somebody may be impersonating him. After another piece of suspense when his life seems to be in danger, the confusion gets worse when Selincourt concludes that he's Bonaparte masquerading as Sir Timothy. Then it's resolved when he hits on the happy expedient of testing him with three questions that only an Englishman could answer. Inevitably the third is about cricket and both men get so carried away by their enthusiasm for it that they forget about the invasion.

The action is over. All that remains are the pleasingly orchestrated farewells, culminating in a beautiful dying fall. Hester, splendid in her golden armour, insists on leaving for East Anglia, accompanied by her maid. Hallam, anxious to have the rest of his evening undisturbed, surprises Humpage with the question Timothy and Lamprett have been firing at him all day: 'Anything to report?' 'Thank God,' he says when the answer comes back negative.

Edward and Dorcas emerge out of the lengthening shadows. In the original version Dorcas speaks a line which Edward takes over in the later version:

> There are times you remember and times you forget, but your life is made up of the times you remember.

The line's rooted far more meaningfully into its context when Dorcas speaks it because she's comparing the memorable day today's been with yesterday, which *looked* very similar.

> The sun shone as it has today, but not so brightly and to no purpose whatever. Yesterday was just – oh, any old day.

She shows him an alcove she played in as a child.

> DORCAS: Yes, it is a good place for us to be together for I have been happy here. It was my world within a world – peopled by folk who were all like me – and that is simple to understand for I was everyone.

John Whiting

> EDWARD: I am a stranger.
> DORCAS: No, no! We all greet you. (*Lightly, she kisses him.*)

Edward makes it clear that he has no interest in life beyond his self-imposed mission. There would be no escape in coming back to Dorcas afterwards. 'I'm only a scarecrow to frighten away the spirit of hatred.' But they love each other now and she carves his name on the seat next to hers. The second version is comparatively prosaic. The words are fewer and the ripples don't spread nearly as far.

> EDWARD: People of my kind get laughed at a lot, you know. There is something comic about the very serious. But, all the same, these questions I ask *are* serious. Mr Matthews is the kind of man who laughs to stop himself from crying. That takes a lot of courage. I've never been able to do it.
> DORCAS: You mustn't ever do that. You must never change.
> EDWARD: I've never cared what people think of me. Somehow I care what you think. (*Pause.*) I must go.

There's more light-hearted fooling about cricket, to dispel any gloom from the atmosphere, and the play ends, as it should, with Hallam and Dorcas together, the brave and beautiful woman, desolated and abandoned, like Catherine at the end of *Marching Song*, together with the philosophizing clown. A song, a spinet inside the house and (only in 1951) Hallam picking up the melody on his recorder.

MARCHING SONG

Whiting himself underrated *Marching Song*. In his interview with *Encore* he said it had no private parts. It may be a more public play than *Saint's Day* but it also draws on his private mythology and it makes its images take on an extraordinary resonance. The city itself becomes unreal, debased, not unlike the village in *Saint's Day*, and Whiting's idealization of his hero Rupert has its roots in his private obsessions, though he integrates all that's needed into the dramatic action. There are less dark corners than in *Saint's Day* but *Marching Song* isn't lacking in virility.

Always better at beginnings than endings, Whiting starts off brilliantly. It's late on a spring evening in Catherine's 'web of glass and steel' set over an unnamed capital. The sky is still savagely bright but shadows have started to form within the room. A man stands on the balcony outside with his back to the room, a stranger at the helm. Harry has just come in but he's already standing there when the curtain goes up, taking his sheepskin coat off. He talks to the man but the man doesn't even turn round. As in Pinter, but four years before *The Room*, there is something outside obscurely threatening the safety of inside the room. The man's presence is obviously a sign that something is about to happen, perhaps happening already. Harry, typically, ignores him once he finds he gets no response and shouts down the stairs to Dido, talking about his vanished youth in the usual Whiting mixture of literary and colloquial language.

> Last Fall – six months ago – I was young and loving. Now, I can only say – welcome. Welcome! Look – but look kindly – on these grey hairs. Trust this ancient head. Will you?
> DIDO: Yes.
> HARRY: That's the girl.
> DIDO: Who's in this place?
> HARRY: Relax. They're friends here.

And like the characters in *A Penny for a Song*, Harry is wryly self-conscious.

> My misery is my dearest possession – for God's sake leave me that.

He uses the fact that Dido is nineteen, nearly twenty, to measure his present self against his past self, and the city, as it is today, against what it was like then.

> HARRY: The day you were born there was music and laughter – and maybe they let off fireworks.
> DIDO: It was a very obscure birth.
> HARRY: But twenty years ago there was music and laughter every day. I know. I was there.

The nostalgic Harry is a good foil for Rupert, who refuses to live in anything but the present. He is later to suggest that all entertainers are romantics: Harry, like most film-makers, is primarily an entertainer. The way he talks tells us a lot about him. All the main characters in *Marching Song*, even Dido, range from the simple-colloquial to the elaborate-rhetorical, but their varieties of rhetoric are well differentiated. Harry's is far the most self-indulgent.

> I'm not young – I've no money – nobody remembers me and the old songs have all gone, but here I am and I'm making a new picture. Twenty years ago I made the picture of my youth. I'll show it to you. Only one copy left. I keep it with me against the dead days. Like an old actor's yellow press-clippings. Baby, look up to me – I once did this!

The fact that he's self-conscious doesn't negate any of the qualities he's self-conscious about.

When the doctor and the priest come in, it becomes still more obvious that something out of the ordinary is afoot: Catherine has sent them out for a walk. This worries Harry, who says he doesn't want his quiet life disturbed. At the same time, their mention of walking to the monument and back helps to substantiate the existence of the city.

With equal economy, Harry's business with the chocolate helps to build up to Catherine's entrance. That Harry carries chocolate in his breast pocket is a good touch. Like him, it's got soft, but Dido eats it and he's fighting with her, ostensibly to get a piece, actually to get a

48

kiss, when Catherine appears in her dressing-gown on the gallery outside her bedroom. When Harry starts talking to the stranger again, Catherine announces her presence by saying he's her new guardian angel, and she sweeps down the stairs.

She gets rid of Dido by sending her down to find the servants (who never appear) and she tells Harry she isn't prepared to go on financing his film and he'll have to go, as will the doctor and the priest. This is not only leading up to saying that Rupert is back, it's also – under great dramatic tension – re-establishing the past for us: planting the point that Rupert has spent seven of his nine years' absence as a prisoner. The mystery of why Doc and Poppa were sent out for a walk is cleared up – to leave her alone to receive Rupert, who now is still upstairs in the bedroom. Believing that he'll stay with her, she feels strong enough to do without the three parasites, though of course she knew all along the film would never be made.

> HARRY: Was there a need to be quite so harsh? I suppose there was. I'd never get out of anywhere nowadays without being pushed out. There's one thing I'd like you to know – not important to you but important to me. It's in you, Kate, that my lamented youth resides. You're the person who represents all that I wanted to be and believed I could be when we first knew each other in the old days. I translated everything – ambition, talent, all values – into your person. I suppose – in my own way, a way you despise – I love you. Don't put up the lights for a minute! (*It is very dark within the room.*)
> CATHERINE: Dry your tears. I'm not looking.
> HARRY: It's just that I hate saying good-bye.
> CATHERINE: The party's over, Harry.

It's getting dark and Rupert, like Catherine, enters quietly on the upstairs gallery in time to overhear Harry's attack on him. It's apt that the light goes on at the beginning of his scene. The romantic gloom of the 'party's over' mood is quickly dispersed as, general-like, he takes command of the situation, coldly polite in face of Harry's obstreperous hostility, while Whiting exploits Harry's romanticism for his own mainly – but not entirely – anti-romantic ends.

> RUPERT: What are you doing here now?
> HARRY: I was making another picture of your beautiful city.

It was to be a sequel to the first picture you remember so well. It was to show how all the pretty little girls of the first picture have become cellar drabs. How the dirty finger of time has pushed in all their sweet little cheeks. It was to show how all the fine young men in their uniforms of the first picture have – well, it was to show that they aren't around any longer.

RUPERT: It sounds most entertaining.

HARRY: Yes, it's the sort of thing would make you laugh a lot.

When Rupert and Catherine are left alone, she describes how Harry arrived penniless six months ago asking her to put him up, and she explains how the three of them were necessary to fill the void created by Rupert's absence. He interrupts to pace out the size of his prison room.

Catherine – that, square, was the exact measurement of my room at the camp. I was sent to that place direct from the freedom of a battlefield. I occupied it for seven years. That little space could have been my childhood nursery, my cadet's room at the military academy, my old battlefields, this room in this house with you – indeed, it could have been any of my particular heavens or hells. Imagination could have made it so. And I could have been any man I wished to be. A free man, if I liked. I chose that the room should be a brick and steel cell in a prison camp in the mountains and that I should be its occupant. A man called Forster.

Again the word 'man' is going to be mentioned a lot as Whiting examines in the scales of dramatic action whether the qualities that raised Rupert above the common level are good or bad. Other things being equal, most of the audience would start off with a natural tendency towards moral disapproval of a German general who served under Hitler. But other things are not equal: we're straight away forced to recognize that at least in his ability to face facts, Rupert is Catherine's superior. But he's also too honest to be tender or kind to her.

It's at this point that the loudspeaker interrupts them, with its hints of 1984 totalitarianism in the democracy that Germany has become, and it prepares the way for the entrance of the Chancellor who is responsible for it, Cadmus.

Each Whiting play has its clown and here the clown is Harry. Like the fool in *Lear*, but at a greater distance of retrospection, he speaks up against the tragic hero with a voice of rather naïve conscience.

> HARRY: Tell me, sir, is your release unconditional? If so, who is our constant companion?
>
> RUPERT: I'm told he's to protect me from annoyance.
>
> HARRY: Then he's not doing his job, is he? Why don't you call him to order?
>
> RUPERT: I've no authority to do that.
>
> HARRY: Authority. That's an interesting word. Are you sure you don't mean power?
>
> RUPERT: No, Mr Lancaster, I mean authority. I have power. Power to throw you down those stairs, for instance. That remains.
>
> HARRY: Would you resort to violence, General?
>
> RUPERT: You're a small man.
>
> HARRY: Has that anything to do with it?
>
> RUPERT: The use of power? Of course, you fool! (*From below the stairs* DIDO *calls:* Harry!) You're being called.
>
> HARRY: All right, honey. I'm talking to what looks like a man. They tell me he's something more, but he looks like a man. I guess the failure to see is in me.

Cadmus's rhetoric is much more polished. The man is perfectly characterized by the way he talks – urbane, ironical, blasé, weary, cynical, self-conscious, distinguished and extremely witty. Like Coriolanus, with whom Harry has compared Rupert, Cadmus despises the common people and the rude facts of ordinary life but, with his usual economy, Whiting establishes this at the same time as building up to something important:

> I find a grave distaste for all food now. For instance, this innocent looking liquid on which I'm compelled to live is actually the glandular secretion of a dying animal. But then, if we were to look too closely at any of our main supports, we'd — (*He stops speaking for a moment and tastes the milk.*) What would happen, Forster? You've had plenty of time to think about such things. Let's have your opinion.

> RUPERT: I'm afraid I can't share your obvious horror of
> material existence.
> CADMUS: You can't? That's a pity.

This is the first, oblique hint of the purpose of the Chancellor's visit
and in developing the story Whiting simultaneously widens the focus
of Cadmus's rather jaundice-coloured lens to give us a picture of the
country as a whole.

> This country has been compelled to accept that system of
> government from the conquerors. It is known as democratic.
> It means that I have an opposition party. This, of course, is a
> great novelty. My opposition party is liberal minded, and they
> have all the savagery possessed by good men. They say it is
> love but they bare their teeth when pronouncing the word. It
> is these men who have brought you back.
> RUPERT: Why?
> CADMUS: We're now an autonomous state again. The occupying
> forces were withdrawn some weeks ago. For seven years we've
> been able to refer our major problems to foreigners. Now, once
> again, as in the war, we're on our own. We have to make up
> our minds about bigger things than the city drainage. One
> of these bigger things, my opposition tells me, is to find out
> who was responsible for this country losing the war. There has
> to be a man, Forster.

The crux of the scene comes when Cadmus intimates that in order to
avoid the mud-slinging of the trial the Opposition demands, Rupert
would be well advised to kill himself. This could be a melodramatic
situation. The suave, knowing, controlled dialogue helps to avert that
danger, and Whiting also makes use of an alienation effect – though
a very un-Brechtian one – to remind us that what we're watching is a
play.

> RUPERT: The result of the trial is a foregone conclusion, then.
> CADMUS: Not at all. If it takes place I shall do everything to
> ensure that it's fairly conducted.
> RUPERT: What do you mean, if it takes place?
> CADMUS: Catherine, a social fact of some importance to you.
> I can allow no one to leave this house for thirty-six hours or

so. No one, that is, except myself. And I must go straightway.
(*He rises.*) I had luncheon with the actor, Constant, today. I
asked him how he would go about telling a man that it was
necessary, indeed imperative, that he should kill himself.

RUPERT: What did he say?

CADMUS: He said drama was, of course, inherent in such a situation for the essence of drama is the dilemma of the central
heroic figure. He was very interesting about that.

After this he doesn't seem at all like a Machiavellian conspirator
as he hands over the box of poison. The tone only becomes slightly
insecure when Whiting again falls into the trap of explaining motives.

CATHERINE: But why, John, why?

CADMUS: Because I cannot allow this trial to take place. I love
this country, Catherine, and I believe that given a few years
I can make it again seem worthy of a place in Europe.
But not if I have this trial forced on me. The mud that is
thrown won't only hit Forster. It will stick to every man,
woman and child of this nation. That is why I will not
allow the trial to take place. That is why Forster must kill
himself.

It would have been better if we hadn't been forced at this stage to
ask whether Cadmus sincerely loves his country and the explicit
emphasis on how the mud would stick to everybody only emphasizes
the weakness of this link in the plot. Playing this speech, Ernest
Thesiger introduced a throb of emotion which assorted oddly with
the sophisticated detachment of the rest of his performance. But the
scene recovers its poise before it finishes:

CATHERINE: You've no authority to give such an order.

CADMUS: It wasn't an order. It was a request. I thought that
was understood.

RUPERT: Perfectly.

CATHERINE: A request. Is that all? Can we do anything else
for you?

CADMUS: Nothing. Will somone help me down? I've a horror of
falling nowadays.

CATHERINE: You're not to touch him, Rupert! You've done
the wrong thing, John. He's safe with me.

John Whiting

CADMUS: Any complete protection – even one of love, Catherine – is also an effective prison. Yes, he's safe with you.

This bridges back very neatly from the political to the personal, though again, after Cadmus has gone, the writing becomes too explicit and a little too self-consciously poetic when Rupert talks to Catherine about the original wearer of the bronze helmet.

I was attempting with my armoured vehicle only to do what he'd tried to do with his armoured head and his antique sword. His end on that field was death, mine was disgrace. But I was left as surely and eternally in that clay-cold earth as was this comrade-in-arms of mine. Our intentions must now be effected by another man in another time: it no longer rests in us. They've taken away the means of achievement, my soldiers. I can't stretch out to the future because I've nothing to use. Cadmus knows that. When I was young I could see far into the future and that makes a man alive. When he cannot see – as at this moment – then a man may as well grant such a request. Cadmus knows I'll do what he asks because there is no future action for me. He knows there is nothing here – nothing anywhere to detain me.

This introduces two themes which are going to be important:
1. different generations of soldiers fighting over the same ground
2. the line of communication from past to future

But the linkage between these two key ideas is perfunctory and the poeticisms like 'clay-cold' mix rather badly with the odd flatness and repetitiveness of the last six sentences. It's good that such an important decision about complying with Cadmus's request should be expressed unemotionally, but this is the wrong sort of flatness.

Robert Flemyng's performance also had the wrong sort of flatness in it. The fact that Whiting himself liked it only proves he had a blind spot somewhere here.

Many people thought the original production lacked warmth, but that was the way I wanted it. The same goes for Robert Flemyng's performance. I admired it very much but it wasn't moving – it wasn't supposed to be.

54

Donald Layne-Smith and Dorothy Tutin as Father Mignon and Sister
Jeanne in *The Devils* at the Aldwych

In the foreground: Diana Wynyard as Catherine, Robert Flemyng as Rupert and Penelope Munday as Dido in the St Martin's production of *Marching Song*

Hartley Power as Harry is at the projector

In a sense, of course, Rupert is dead already when the play begins, but if he's entirely dead, there's no drama. We have to see some residue of the man Rupert was before the massacre of the children and we have to sense a great tension. Robert Flemyng was altogether too wooden. Gustaf Gründgens, who played the part in Düsseldorf, injected an extraordinarily exciting tension in it, without ever coming too much to life. We could still believe he'd been in prison for seven years. Unfortunately the surrounding performances were flabby, whereas in London, Diana Wynyard was at her best as Catherine and neither Penelope Munday nor Hartley Power could have been better as Dido and Harry.

Of course, Rupert's big speech doesn't end the act. Whiting is too good a technician for that. Dido comes back, and at the worst possible moment, just after Rupert has explicitly told Catherine he's no longer in love with her. But the brief sequence which takes us to the curtain is very funny, especially when Dido talks about Harry.

> He talked about God, social injustice – he cried a little there – war and love of mankind. What he meant, of course, was love of his own kind.

And when she tells Rupert about her previous encounters with soldiers. The curtain line

> DIDO: Well, with those men on the door it looks as if I'll be here for a time.

isn't a curtain line at all in the accepted sense. Effectively, the act ends with the look between Dido and Rupert, which should indicate not sexual attraction but curiosity.

Act Two begins with a *coup de théatre*. The curtain goes up on a stage which is dark except for the light from Harry's film projector as he screens the film of his youth. We see only the tail end of the film and as the lights go up we see Dido sitting on the floor asleep with her head resting against Rupert's knees. Catherine, instead of looking at the screen, is watching her, as she must have been during the film. Only one line of dialogue has so far been spoken – 'Will somebody put up the lights?' All these points are made visually and the first sequence of dialogue is devoted amusingly to Harry's mortified

E

John Whiting

discovery that Dido has been asleep and her typically honest reactions to what she saw.

> The young ones look sort of muddy – and don't they grin a lot? Was there so much to laugh about in those days? (*She suddenly looks round at the others.*) I suppose all of you were young at that time.

Whiting doesn't aim at a thorough-going realism in her language any more than Shakespeare tries to make a grave-digger or a fourteen-year-old girl in Verona speak as they would 'in real life', but Whiting, like Shakespeare, mixes realism into his rhetoric, and with Dido he was even slightly ahead of his time. Her lines still sound oddly cool and contemporary for a play set in 1952.

Another Shakespearean characteristic in Whiting – both playwrights were actors – is the way that so much stage business is implied in the dialogue. There's a good example of this in the scene where Rupert helps Harry to pack away the screen and the projector. It's impossible to read through the passage in the script without forming a mental picture of the blocking – Harry pursuing Rupert and trying to get a straight look into his eyes, Rupert purposefully going on with rolling up the screen and moving things about the stage to evade and interrupt the direct line of questions Harry is firing at him.

> DIDO: Why did you show it tonight?
> HARRY: I thought – wrongly, of course – that it might relax the tension for a couple of hours. I thought it'd give Kate something to look at beside you two. You'll forgive me asking this: what the hell are you up to?
> RUPERT: Where do you want this?
> (*He refers to the cinema screen.*)
> HARRY: I'll take it down with me. For God's sake, Forster, couldn't you have kept this sort of thing until we were all let out of this place? I know you've been shut up for seven years, but you could surely have waited a while longer. Until you could have got this – this girl out of here. Away from Kate.
> RUPERT: Anything else I can do? With this stuff, I mean.

HARRY: Not a thing. Do you think since you came back last
night you've been playing fair?

RUPERT: Fair?

HARRY: Look. I'll try to explain. Don't you think it would
have been better to pretend for a while? Pretend with Kate
that everything is just as it has been. Christ, man, you're
breaking her heart! Is that simple enough for you?

RUPERT: There! Everything packed. You can go down.

Rupert is only direct with him when Harry accuses him of wanting
to start another war.

HARRY: What are they going to do – suddenly release you into
an unsuspecting world as the latest saviour? If so, I take cover.
Who's the enemy going to be this time? Or haven't you
decided yet?

RUPERT: I have to act on my decisions, Lancaster. Unlike you
I don't make up my mind and regard it as an end in itself.

HARRY: Me! I'm just an old dreamy-eyes. But I don't murder.

RUPERT: When you have you'll find it simpler to tell the innocent
from the guilty.

Whiting doesn't find it at all easy to tell the innocent from the
guilty or the good from the bad. He lets Harry make out a very
convincing case against Rupert, which is by no means invalidated by
its coming from Harry. He may be a fool, but as Cadmus says later,
his opinions are those of the 'ordinary people'. The hostility of the
ordinary people is not one of the main factors that drive Rupert to
suicide, but it's not irrelevant to the more important point that there's
no future for him. Whiting obviously admires Rupert and doesn't
admire Harry, but the moral distinction between the two kinds of
men isn't a simple one. Harry does less damage than Rupert, but he's
less honest and less capable of accepting responsibility.

Rupert is a professional soldier and unlike Edward Sterne he
doesn't rebel against his profession. He tries to go on but he gets
caught by a moment of human feeling. Like Paul, he undergoes a
conversion and as in *Saint's Day* it's too late. He's already blown the
child's brains out and signalled to his tank commanders to move
forward over the children who are getting in the way. But he can't
go on. His unconscious passes sentence on him and condemns him

to failure and imprisonment by making him hesitate too long on the wrong side of the river. His suicide is a logical continuation of the same line of action. It's not a moral act, it's a practical consequence. Interested as he is in moral issues, Whiting never makes things happen for moral reasons. He states the issues objectively, asking the right questions (some of them through Harry) and he lets things work themselves out according to the remorseless logic of tragic action.

It's Dido who states the alternatives that confront Rupert, justly and perceptively.

> So what are you going to do? Live in retirement? Say, a house in the country, your feet up of an evening, early to bed. You'll be healthy all right, but I've doubts as to your wealth and wisdom. What else? You'll be able to walk round your estate in the morning and again in the evening. If you get very bored perhaps you could shoot a small animal every so often. Do I make the prospect sound attractive?
>
> RUPERT: No.
>
> DIDO: I wasn't trying to. As an alternative you might make it up with Catherine, stay on here, and – as Harry suggested – pretend.
>
> RUPERT: I'm not good at that.
>
> DIDO: No good at pretending! Then I'd say your future is about as bright as a blind man's holiday.

It's ironic that she should say this without knowing what Cadmus has asked Rupert to do and it's also ironic that a girl who argues like this has the effect of making him want to live. That she senses she's pivotal to some important decision is unrealistic but theatrically effective and consistent with Whiting's policy of making his characters ultra-conscious.

> DIDO: You're about to make some kind of confession to me. Well, don't do it. I don't want to hear.
>
> RUPERT: Very well.
>
> DIDO: I don't want to get mixed up. I don't want to have any influence on what you think or do or say. I'm free! and I want to stay like that. It's been very nice and interesting talking to you, but now I must be getting back.

RUPERT: To what? Somebody down in the city? Are you in love?

DIDO: That's the point. I'm not. I've told you, I'm free and I want to stay free.

RUPERT: What's the danger here?

DIDO: Oh, don't be such a bloody fool! You are. (RUPERT *laughs*.) It's not funny! Think of Catherine. For seven years she's been shut up in her love for you. Everything she has done – everything she has thought and believed has been decided by that love. Was it worth it? I don't think so. She may get free again in time – she's brave, you can see that – but life's too short, too damned short for these stretches of hard labour.

This links up with Cadmus's image of love as an effective prison.

Catherine too is unnaturalistically perceptive. Very few women who'd seen what she has seen would try to persuade Dido to stay in the house, but it's rather moving when she does.

CATHERINE: He likes you very much so won't you stay on?

DIDO: No.

CATHERINE: For tonight, at least.

DIDO: No. I want to go home.

CATHERINE: Is there something urgent calling you back?

DIDO: No. I just want to get out of here.

CATHERINE: Please stay. For my sake.

DIDO: For you?

CATHERINE: Yes.

DIDO: I'll stay for you.

CATHERINE: You funny girl. Do you make a habit of the unexpected? Anyway, thank you.

The terse, pebble-hard lines obviate the danger of over-emotionality at the same time as making it easier for us to credit it that Dido would do this for Catherine. And after seeing this, we believe Catherine when she tells Harry she's not fighting to keep anything for herself. Rupert is once again touched by her warmth. Nothing could make him change his attitude to her but it does make him apologize for it.

CATHERINE: Rupert, it's not a sign of weakness to have someone with you through these hours. Why be afraid of showing that you're human? It's a failing the rest of us admit. Why not

> you? There have been times in the past when I've been able to
> comfort you. I don't remember them as moments of weakness.
> RUPERT: Catherine, I didn't want it to end like this with you.
> Believe that. But I had to tell you.

Again the stress on the word *human* almost suggests Rupert is trying
to be superhuman.

As in *Saint's Day*, where the suspense is heightened by making us
wait for a call from another room which will somehow alter the
status quo, here we're in suspense waiting for Dido to say something
which will alter Rupert's decision.

> RUPERT: Why should she be involved?
> CATHERINE: Yet you want her to stay. You watch her. You
> wait for her to speak. What do you hope to hear?
> RUPERT: I don't know.
> CATHERINE: Something that can never come from me. So I
> asked her to stay. She may casually – without any thought at
> all – help you.
> RUPERT: I think it's unlikely.

But he knows it's possible.

Despite all the obvious differences of generation, class, experience
and outlook between Rupert and Dido, they have two basic things in
common. They are both honest and both have remained uncommitted.
Rupert describes his past profession to her in terms of an Irish
'predecessor in war'.

> All the business of war, and indeed all the business of life, is
> to endeavour to find out what you don't know by what you do . . .
> That's what I called 'guessing what was at the other side of the
> hill'.

If Rupert had committed himself to loving Catherine, he'd have seen
the other side of the hill with eyes not entirely his own, while Dido
has kept her freedom simply because she enjoys living in the present
– singing and dancing and lying in the sun – and because she's never
felt strong enough to take on the responsibilities of loving someone.
Her description of the time she most nearly fell in love involves a
blind soldier.

60

Nobody – not even the proudest person – knows when their cry
for help goes out. It may not even be spoken by you. When I
was a kid there was a boy and he went to the war. He came back
from the fighting earlier than was expected. I went to meet him
at the East Railway Station, and it was there the trap was sprung.
He'd come back without his eyes. I cut myself loose from that one
easily enough, but as I get older it's more difficult. Everywhere
I go there are the unhappy and the aimless waiting for me to put
out my hand and walk into that trap made of human arms. Ach!
this loving business.

She understands the arrogance implicit in thinking personal freedom
worth preserving. His objective has been to impose himself, to 'reach
a point of achievement never before known by man'. This was his
tragic hubris and it gets established just before his speech about the
incident that caused his downfall. As in *Conditions of Agreement*, a
single incident from the past, involving death, is described at length
because it has turned out to be crucial in determining the future.

Whiting, like Hemingway, was fascinated by all aspects of warfare,
and the account of Rupert's strategy in the battle is a convincing one,
however different his rhetoric from the average general's. But the
satisfaction he gets out of success is much more that of the aesthete.

My intention was to go in at dawn and take the town at my
leisure through the day, but at dusk, with the full weight of my
force, to establish two bridgeheads over the river and attempt a
crossing that night: on the supposition that the enemy would
expect a break between the attack on the town and the river
crossing. You understand? It was to be a very beautiful battle,
having an elegance difficult to achieve with the use of armoured
forces.

And as in a good novel, the sharp vividness of the incident in Rupert's
memory is captured by a clear delineation of individual moments.
Coming out of the church and standing on the steps, the little boy
puts his hand to his mouth as if eating a sweet but instead blows a
whistle. Some of the boys who come rushing out of the church and
out of the houses and down the street carry flags.

The boy who had come first from the church had clambered on
to my tank. He was black-haired and black-eyed and he carried

61

a wooden sword which he swung above his head. He shouted something which I didn't understand, and then spat at me. That was no provocation for what I did: I had already decided. I stretched out and drew his head to my shoulder like a lover, and shot him in the mouth. I took him by the hair of his shattered head and held him up for my men to see. They understood. The shooting began. They also used knives to cut them free from the armour. The note of the children's cry changed and was in mercy drowned as the motors started up and we moved forward.

'In mercy drowned' is a rather literary inversion but it does nothing to interfere with the force of the passage. The whole speech lasts over two minutes and the impact is enormous. The town, the river, the church, the tank, the wooden sword, the child's shattered head are none of them symbols but they have a resonance as images which go beyond their function as elements in the narrative. As in *A Penny for a Song*, the involvement of children in a battle makes the ghastliness of it stand out in sharp relief. Like Brecht, Whiting was simultaneously revolted and fascinated by the cruelties of warfare.

After the unrelieved tension of this scene, Cadmus's wit, when he comes up with Catherine, serves usefully as comic relief and the confrontation between the suave old diplomat and the outspoken young girl is very funny.

CADMUS: There is an old-fashioned idea that extreme youth and, if I may say so, beauty —
DIDO: I'm not beautiful.
CADMUS: No, you're not. I'm so sorry. Never mind. Perhaps you are clever, instead. Are you?
DIDO: No.
CADMUS: Oh, dear! Neither beautiful nor clever. You're kindhearted, that's what it is. That's the gift God gave you. To understand your fellow beings.
DIDO: That's it.
CADMUS: Catherine – Forster, will one of you disengage me from this conversation, please.

But the scene between Rupert and Cadmus when Dido goes is not so good. In order to get points across to us, Whiting makes Rupert say things to Cadmus that he wouldn't say to Cadmus. All Cadmus needs to know from him is what he intends to do. All he needs to know from Cadmus is what will happen if he refuses to kill himself. Cadmus explains

> CADMUS: You'll be taken to the military prison in the city. The place the soldiers laughingly call Arcady.* I shall make a statement that you are there and that you are to be tried. The process of law will be set in motion. As the trial proceeds you'll be forgotten, and all we shall be aware of will be the rotting corpse of the country covered by the ordure of our recent history.

When Cadmus asks Rupert to make up his mind, it's very hard to accept what he says in reply as belonging to this conversation at all.

> RUPERT: My last positive action – by my decision – was the murder of that child seven years ago. From that moment I not only relinquished command of my army, but also of myself. For the seven years in prison I lived by other men's decisions regarding my habits, my actions and my thoughts. I did what I was told. Nothing more. I was content it should be like that. Soldiers, you know, are forced to action by their decisions. There's no getting out of it for men in my job. No going back and saying I didn't mean it, when in my hand I'm holding the casualty list for thousands. You'll forgive my contempt for men who think they've fulfilled their obligations by expressing an opinion.

The efforts to develop the theme of the line of communication, interesting though this idea is, is also slightly laboured. Rupert is too transparently expounding his present situation and the line of dramatic tension has gone too slack.

The same trouble continues into the three-handed dialogue when Harry invades the scene. Instead of leaving the characters quite enough rein to follow their own courses, Whiting harnesses them to advancing the points he wants to make.

> HARRY: Because he's a man, I guess. Beneath the splendour, you know – (*he is beside the bronze helmet: he taps it with his*

* Whiting is fond of these names with classical echoes – Arcady, Cadmus, de Troyes – but not too much should be read into this.

fist) – empty. Hollow. Nothing. Nothing but a man signalling
to be let out of the trappings of war. Asking to be taken back
into the herd.

CADMUS: Is that so, Forster?

RUPERT: Lancaster has a liberal mind. To him no man is
entirely evil. Not even me. And so he is compelled to mistake
my gestures of defiance for signals of distress.

The contrasts between the two opposed attitudes become too schematic. The play only recovers momentum when Cadmus, a much
more accomplished *metteur-en-scene* than Stella, 'rouses the rabble' in
Harry, making him speak out in the voice of the rabble against
Rupert.

That kind break more than hearts. They're not often caught as
you've caught this one, and you don't often see the naked face
out of its idiot covering. Don't let it go free.

After this the action speeds up considerably and the dialogue
between Rupert and Dido which ends the act is on the same high
level as their earlier dialogue. She comes back from seeing Cadmus
down the stairs, angry that he should have said it is because of her
that Rupert has decided to face the trial. He tells her it's entirely his
own decision but when she hears that afterwards he'll be allowed to
go free, she falls right into the trap that she's so sedulously been
avoiding. She's like a non-malignant Hilde Wangel who snares herself
instead of her Master Builder.

DIDO: And when it's all over?

RUPERT: They'll let me go.

DIDO: To be old and angry and lonely. No!

RUPERT: You mustn't concern yourself. Keep free.

DIDO: All right. I love you, if that's what you want to hear me
say. I love you. You seem to me a very good man.

He talks to her about soldiering, describing what it's like to wait
for dawn to break on the morning of a battle and again there's hubris
when he tells her about the feelings he had, staring into the darkness.

Towards the end of the campaign I almost came to believe that
it was the intensity of my vision which dispelled the night

and the strength of my faith which lifted the sun into the sky.

His insistent 'I'm sane, you know' is like Grandier's asking the Sewerman whether he's mad just before launching into the speech about creating God. But the substance of this scene in *Marching Song* is much more solid than its counterpart in *The Devils*.

Then, in the last few seconds of the act, we get a new clue to what it is about soldiering that makes it so appealing.

> DIDO: Would you like to roll up and sleep for a while? I'll watch. Oh, come on. I'm not such a fool. You've trusted people before me. Rest. I'll watch. Sleep.
> RUPERT: Yes, you have to trust someone. That's the comradeship of soldiering. The knowledge that you're a man. And need to be watched over in the last hours of the night. Protected. From hurt. And death.

At moments like this the hero is on a par with the herd. Just a man.

It's impossible to say exactly when Rupert decides to kill himself. In Act Three, just after daybreak, Cadmus says that he gave the orders 'some hours ago' for Rupert's death to be announced at dawn though when he left in Act Two he told Dido on the stairs that Rupert had decided to live. We can only take it that he said this for the sake of what he thought it would make her say to Rupert. At the beginning of Act Three he still intends to live. 'I want the present time as offered by John Cadmus.' The first sign we get that he's changed his mind is when he makes Dido a present of the jewelled box which contained the poison. So somewhere between these two points the decision is taken.

Harry's emotionally extravagant gesture in burning the only surviving copy of his film is a kind of clownish parallel to the suicide. Rupert has needed a life-line to survive; Harry has needed a life-lie – he'll now have to stop thinking of himself as a great director. But whereas Rupert's suicide is clean and makes no emotional demands on anyone else, Harry's gesture is messy and only causes trouble for other people. The doctor is hauled out of bed to dress his burns and Catherine has to ask Dido to go down to see him – which leaves

John Whiting

Catherine alone with Rupert till Cadmus arrives with Bruno Hurst. It's only a brief scene they have together but it shows how much the action of the play has changed her. When Rupert remarks à propos of Harry how dangerous it is to distort the world around you to satisfy your longing, she retorts:

> There's more danger, you know, in trying to destroy it to satisfy your ambition. You made me say that. I don't want to drag up the past any more. The damnable part of it is that men of your kind shatter the ordinary, everyday human pride of people like me.
>
> RUPERT: By that you're at last seeing me as I am.
> CATHERINE: I believe so.

Cadmus takes Catherine downstairs to leave Rupert alone with Bruno, the twenty-two-year-old guard commander. When he hears Bruno has been stationed in the Eastern Provinces, Rupert talks to him about the goat-songs, which formed his life-line, and finds out that they aren't songs of prayer, as he thought, but obscene songs of love for the goats. It would be wrong to take this literally as a major factor in causing Rupert's change of mind about the suicide, but it's a sign of the dawning realization that, just as the line of communication which led him from the past into the present wasn't a valid one, there's no valid one from the present into the future. There's no function, no life left for him.

That Bruno used to play 'Forster's game' as a child is very germane to developing the theme of different generations of soldiers fighting over the same ground. Rupert has had to face the same problems as the men who wore the bronze helmet. Bruno hasn't yet had to fight but playing the game he found it agony not to carry on with the attack over the river and he believes that if he'd gone through the same experience, he could have gone on. Possibly he will be called on to fight.

In the confessional speech to him, Rupert makes several new points:

> I couldn't free myself from that moment. The moment when I stood alone, sad, lost, childless, with the child in my arms. And looking down saw that it was a human being. Warm, as

the bitter smell of its body struck up at me: dirty, fearful, brave and – living. It was then the secret was forced on me. I'd shut it out until that morning by making my own prison, Hurst, years before they sent me to the camp in the mountains. A prison of pride and ambition. Then, when I caught the child to me, the secret was revealed. I suddenly understood what a man is. For I held it close.

BRUNO: If you felt this why did you shoot?

RUPERT: I had no choice. The way I'd chosen to live led to that encounter, which was in itself a challenge. Are you so great? Then fire! I fired, and the secret flew up leaving only blood on my sleeve. I became human. So I waited.

Childlessness is the price he's paid for refusing to commit himself to marriage with Catherine. The secret is one simply of humanity and it's eluded him in all this time of pride. Killing the child, he underwent a conversion, like Robert in killing Stella, but his conversion, like Paul's is in the opposite direction. He frees himself from the prison of anti-social pride and egoistic ambition. For Rupert the way is from prison to prison to death. The moment of existential choice was the moment when the child was in his arms. But he wasn't free to choose. As a soldier, he had to kill and advance. Having done so, as a man, he couldn't go on. This is the crux of the play and no one but Whiting could have worked it out like this.

As before, he structures the sequence of moods so that a grave moment like this is followed by a relief of tension. Dido's encounter with Bruno is amusing, but, as with so many lines in the last act of *Saint's Day*, there's also a casual hint of the death which is now so imminent. When Bruno says there are to be eight soldiers in the escort, her comment is:

> Enough to carry you away if necessary with full military honours.

BRUNO: We're an escort, ma'am, not a bearer party.

She laughs at Bruno for calling her madam and when he says he just obeys orders she teases him by ordering him to leave the room. But she also makes an important moral point in between jokes. 'Are you doing the right thing?' she asks explicitly, making him answer, explicitly, 'That doesn't concern me.' He's a soldier. Like Melrose and like concentration camp guards, he leaves the responsibility with his superiors.

In Harry's scene too, comedy is interwoven with moral comment. The accident has made Harry look like the clown he's always been. The burns on one side of his face have been treated with a brightly coloured dye and his hands are bandaged. He's also very drunk. But he talks about being a man and his unsubtle insistence that his way of life's right and Rupert's wrong has an added meaning because of what Rupert has said just before he came in.

> The whole way you've gone is'n insult to what y'could be.

But Harry himself is more pathetic than ever and admits that he made the gesture to arouse sympathy.

Cadmus calls Bruno away in order to give Rupert time and opportunity to kill himself. It also provides a chance for farewell scenes with Catherine and Dido, who both think he's leaving for 'Arcady' – the choice of name has an ironic double meaning here.

Parting from Dido, Rupert gives her good advice, which at the end of the play she's going to ignore.

> Don't stay caught in the memory of the past day. Escape. Get out.

And when she holds out her hand, he takes it with his left, which tells us he's holding the poison behind his back with his right.

The actual death, though off-stage, as in classical tragedy, is still stunningly theatrical. Rupert has no sooner gone up to the bedroom than the public address system is heard for the second time.

> The time is zero four one five hours. The time is zero four one five hours. It is now – officially – Day. (*A bell is struck. The man on the balcony enters the room, crosses, and goes down the stairs.* THE ANNOUNCER *speaks again.*) Attention! Here is a statement. General Rupert Forster is dead. General Rupert Forster is dead. Further reports follow later.

Dido is transfixed. Catherine rushes in and makes her go up to the bedroom. Cadmus has already come up the stairs by the time she reappears with the news that it's true. And Whiting writes such good rhetoric for Cadmus here that most of what he says – related though it is to a cold, objective assessment of the political situation – has a strong undertone of affection and admiration for Rupert which makes the speech work almost like a funeral oration.

> I knew him as a man to be very much like myself. But he'd something I've had to put away whilst I'm in office. Honour. So I knew what the end would be. . . . We're all victims of injustice, Catherine, every moment of our lives. We can shut ourselves up in the day and lie awake at night dreaming of revenge. But revenge against whom? Against each other? Why? Forster had great cause to dream in that way. It was an injustice that we had to imprison him, and he had reason to sit in that camp in the hills thinking up ways of reckoning. But he didn't do that. All he wanted was to be taken back into the service of the world. The world wouldn't have him and so he turned away. In acceptance. There was no hatred in him. He was a great soldier. Learn from him.

His death produces a catharsis in which there's more than a hint of possible new growth. Cadmus will have to make a lying statement to the House, so he can't afford to learn, but Catherine has learnt a lot and Dido is now learning what Catherine had predicted she would learn.

> Quite soon now the day will come when you'll have to admit that the anger and despair you feel is not because of other people. It is for them.

When Dido sacrifices her liberty at the end of the play to stay on in the house with Catherine, it shows that day has come – a consciously sentimental decision from the girl who'd resisted sentiment so fiercely and after being so honest about everything, she now lies to Catherine about a last message from Rupert saying he loved her. But at least she'll save Catherine from Harry and the hangers-on.

THE GATES OF SUMMER

The Gates of Summer was written in 1953 and produced in 1956, opening at the New Theatre Oxford in September. Peter Hall directed, with James Donald as John Hogarth, Isabel Jeans as Sophie Faramond, and Lionel Jeffries as Henry Bevis. Dorothy Tutin's understudy, Jocelyn James, played Caroline Traherne on the first night and subsequently when Dorothy Tutin had to go to hospital. There would have been time to replace her before bringing the play into London, but it never came in.

Whiting described it as the harshest play he'd written, although it's a comedy. Certainly it's the most cynical, always humorous but acidly disillusioned and disillusioning. If the original *A Penny for a Song* was written, as he said, in 'a period of great personal happiness', *The Gates of Summer* is obviously the product of deep disenchantment. The characters aren't conceived with the same comic detachment as in *A Penny for a Song*. *The Gates of Summer* is a comedy chiefly in the sense that the characters all fall short of tragedy. John aims at a hero's death fighting for the freedom of Greece; Caroline aims at dying together with her lover, but things don't pan out as they've planned them. The bubbles are blown up only to be pricked.

John has cut loose from all his ties in England to join a rebellion, which turns out to be not a popular movement but an abortive reactionary conspiracy, staged by a handful of aristocrats. Not understanding this, John hands over a cheque for £100,000 to Prince Basilios to finance the movement: the old man spends it all on an elaborate garden party, trying to charge for admission, but no one comes except the woman he loves – and the party was her idea. The characters all act out their impulses extravagantly but unlike the characters in *A Penny for a Song*, they aren't eccentric or obsessional or endearing. They're activated by an overwhelming urge to resolve their conflicts, and fail because the conflicts are too big and they're too small. They then find it easier to forgive each other than forgive themselves, and of course they're right.

The action is set in the early summer of 1913 – this time just before, not just after, a world war. Again we're in a room in a country house outside a European capital – Athens this time – and again the house is high up. It stands above a valley. Again there's a struggle between two women of different generations over a man. Sophie is in her fifties; Caroline is twenty-five. And again exile is a main theme. Sophie left England when she left John, marrying Selwyn, an archaeologist, like Dido's father. John 'bought a state of exile' by selling everything he had in England and breaking off an affair with a bishop's wife. He made the break on his thirty-fifth birthday.

> When it was done, I felt remarkable. Sanctified. I had nothing in the world but money.

The play starts, like *Conditions of Agreement*, with the arrival of a man at the house of a woman he hasn't seen for a very long time. It's ten years since Sophie left him. That too was on a birthday.

> I awoke very much alone . . . Then your gift was brought to me. Ah! you were still young enough at that time to give me birthday presents without flinching. I took off the wrappings and there was the musical box. Something to be given to a child – or to me. I opened the lid and the music began. And with the music the tears. I knew then it was time to go.

Now, like Catherine, she's caught up in the memory of the past. She's dictating her memoirs, but John figures on every page of them. He's already become a real and important man to Cristos, who's writing from Sophie's dictation, and to Caroline, Selwyn's daughter, who's here recovering from the disaster of a marriage 'contracted' (as if it were a disease) when she was seventeen.

The first act is fairly static, given over to elaborate character analyses, protracted reminiscences, and narrative speeches which resurrect the past, like so many interconnected short stories. So Sophie and Caroline discuss John at length. Sophie doesn't know that Caroline, bribing Cristos by letting him kiss her, has gained access to the book. In it Sophie has described John as the first twentieth-century man:

> He was the only man I knew who seemed perfectly unequipped to face the future. I knew he'd survive . . . the qualities needed

for survival as a person are the same unsocial qualities which can destroy an individual, a community or even a country. So the lack of moral equipment of the genius and the great criminal are much the same. It's what you haven't got that matters. John's great strength was that he lacked seriousness.

Caroline sees hope for herself in the loss of faith that she hopes he will bring her. She is like a predatory female Procathren bearing down on a handsome nihilist.

Between the weak wail of arrival and the whimper of departure there's no cause for alarm but cause for laughter. Can I see it that way – with him – through him?

But Sophie thinks that with his new commitment to revolution, John must be more serious now.

The parallels and contrasts between the characters and their stories are just slightly too neat, bordering on the schematic.

JOHN: I'm also running away from a marriage. Not my own. Someone else's.
CAROLINE: He just went into hiding. From what I hear, you're making for the open country.
JOHN: I hope so.
CAROLINE: You're looking for more than the heroism of love.
JOHN: I'd say the stoicism of love.
CAROLINE: Liberation.
JOHN: Of others. Not myself.

We again think of *Saint's Day* when we hear John has incurred the hostility of the mob. The bishop has forgiven him for the affair with his wife. (Up to *The Devils*, Whiting's many clerics all seem to be victims of circumstances, very willing to forgive others.) But Ada had made a confession to a national newspaper and an angry crowd had thrown stones at his window. 'They'd got it into their heads that I was breaking something very dear to their hearts: a home.'

This theme of conflict between the hero and the mob is dealt with much more perfunctorily than it is in *Saint's Day*, though the plays are basically concerned with the same interrelated subjects of exile, isolation and self-destruction. In *The Gates of Summer* Whiting is much more inclined to handle themes just by letting the characters talk about them.

JOHN: All the best games end in destruction.
CAROLINE: We never get out of the nursery, where everything finishes broken up. You played the whole of your life in London that way, didn't you? Without seriousness, because you knew the time would come when you'd have to put your toys away. So better smash them! You were quite right . . . If I'd seen my marriage with Boysie – and the break-up – as you saw your love affairs, then I wouldn't have been unhappy.

The incident of the mob's stoning John's house because of his adultery is not the only one in *The Gates of Summer* that's hard to believe in. It's hard to accept John as an ex-Member of Parliament, even in 1913. Laconically he tells us 'Some years ago my friends wanted me to get settled. Before I knew what was happening I found myself to be an M.P.' And he made his maiden speech about 'the government's attitude to this minority group under Basilios in the North'. It's also hard to believe that *The Times* would send out a full-time correspondent to cover a dig like Selwyn's and although virtually nothing has yet been found, Henry Bevis has been writing a column about it every fortnight. Asked how he fills the space he says, 'It's the suspense, Selwyn.'

Henry Bevis's function in the action is partly as a pathetic clown, like Harry, who parallels the hero in many ways and rivals him unsuccessfully for the affections of a woman. John makes a strong impression on Caroline without trying. Henry tries incessantly and much too hard.

CAROLINE: Why should you help me?
HENRY: I cling to that as the one definite aim I have.

He advises her to read poetry.

Talking about the feeling he has of coming alive in Greece, John shows that he's one of the many characters in Whiting who feel a distaste for the physical realities of human existence.

Aware that you're here! Alive, wound up – more! – working, ticking, going. Registering something more than a mood. Yes . . .

73

John Whiting

> Life isn't after all founded on the meal table, the privy and the bed.

And Selwyn's patronizing, detached superiority is sometimes reminiscent of Cadmus's tone in his talk of playing music over the public address system to wash away grievances:

> Nothing like digging and sifting for keeping the mind off sex . . . When I was in the army and it became troublesome, I'd always call a church parade. Made the men rather unhappy turning out so late at night, but it always worked.

Like Whiting's other heroes, John tries to rise above himself.

> CAROLINE: Good food, sleep, the comfort of women are gone in this Spartan search for an absolute truth in a harsher reality. Great man – nearly a saint, you are – yes – for the way of sanctity is the road to the North.
>
> JOHN: . . . The pleasures you've talked about have become as bitter to me as any penance. For they're only tolerable when they're more than themselves.

This is not only too explicit, it makes John too much of a mouthpiece for the attitude which rejects the ordinary satisfactions rather in the way Celia embodies it in *The Cocktail Party*.

As in *Saint's Day* and *A Penny for a Song*, the play is centred partly on a sequence of action which is off-stage: the dig becomes very important. Just as Selwyn thinks he's on the brink of a major discovery, a workman falls through a hole into some kind of underground cavern and, instead of replying rationally to questions shouted at him from above, he wanders about, laughing uproariously. An extra off-stage diversion is provided by the foreman's marriage. Two hundred relations are invited. They roast sheep and dance under the hill. Sophie and Selwyn go down to join in the celebration and Henry comes in and out reporting on what he's seen. Whiting contrives it all very neatly but it would have been much better in a film because it's not the sort of action that gains from being treated at a remove.

In some ways John is like a combination of Rupert and Dido. When he tells Caroline 'I've always been aware of the perils of travel and you're one of them' he sounds like Dido fighting to avoid the

74

trap that's 'made of human arm's. And his on-stage life, like Rupert's, is bedevilled by the need to make a choice involving death, honour and a woman. Either he can stay with Caroline or go North to what sounds as though it would be a noble death. (Altogether John is rather Byronic and he's almost the same age Byron was when he was killed – thirty-six.) But he's promised to go and he avoids becoming a tragic hero only because he's not allowed to act on his decisions, as Rupert was.

Whiting's view of women becomes progressively more bitter. The 1962 Dorcas is far less amiable than her 1951 counterpart. Sophie has some of Catherine's wit but none of her nobility. Caroline is engaging but almost as dangerous as Soeur Jeanne. She has almost caused Henry's death by 'translating' for him and describing him to a group of Greek horsemen as a rich Turkish merchant interested in buying Greek girls. So when he offers money to them they attack him and, like so many of Whiting's clowns, he gets 'lacerated and bruised mercifully beyond recognition for several days'. Only this time we don't see him in his mutilated state.

And like the goat-song in *Marching Song*, which Rupert had believed to be a song of prayer, the underground cavern turns out to be obscene. Selwyn, who had expected it to be a place of worship finds bas reliefs all over the walls representing figures celebrating endless love rites. When she sees them, Caroline tells John 'You and I have learnt nothing new in two thousand years.' Like warriors, different generations of lovers can only repeat each other.

The part of the play which has dated most in the fifteen years since it was written is the quandary Henry finds himself in about how to describe the 'golden lovers' in language suitable for readers of *The Times*. He goes to John, who at the time thinks he's dying from Caroline's poisoned berries, to ask his advice, and, in a lyrical bravura of irony, John dictates a report for Henry to send in about the ideal woman.

> For she was born for many of us among the raspberry bushes on a hot afternoon in the garden when the younger children laughed and played, but you and I, sir, older (at least fourteen) silent, horribly wiser stayed out of sight . . . born in the fevered head on that torrid day with the sun falling out of the sky. She stayed with you growing in beauty and experience as your imagination

and longing swept you into manhood . . . She was so nearly met. There was always the chance of absolute discovery in so many encounters. And yet. And yet.

Where was she? . . . she was with you until you lost your ambition. Yes, sir, age is responsible for too much. That's agreed. It's responsible, you'll remember, for the loneliness which made you make do with that angel in tweeds across the breakfast table. She's kind to dogs . . . Soon she'll go from the room and pat you on the head as she passes. If you're lucky.

Your Correspondent wishes to send a message of hope to the unloved . . . Yet wait . . . With the message of hope must come a warning.

Ah! sir, in two thousand years she has not aged. Her bed is still a jousting ground: yours is now a place of rest. Her way of adoration has not become a good-night kiss pecked into the forehead. There are other differences too painful for this journal to print.

The one theme in *The Gates of Summer* in which Whiting hadn't previously seemed so interested is the discrepancy between the myth of a man's life and its reality. This is just touched on in *Marching Song* when, immediately after Rupert's death, Cadmus talks about going down to tell lies to the House, belittling Forster's past achievements and saying that he died under a burden of conscience. The treatment of the John Hogarth myth is much more complex. The past John Hogarth is different from the man we see and Sophie's memory of him is different from the reality. What she dictates to Cristos probably doesn't tally exactly with what she remembers and what he writes down certainly doesn't tally with what she dictates – he's intent on building up a myth – though when she reads it, she doesn't realize how he's departed from what she said. At the end, Sophie refuses to give Caroline any part in the book, notwithstanding the part she's played in John's life. Like Catherine, who didn't want to hear weekly reports of Rupert's growing older and sadder in the prison camp, Sophie is more interested in keeping her own image of John intact. She also turns out to be a historian who's quite willing to interfere with history. She sends a telegram to *The Times*, signed Henry Bendix, reporting John's death fighting in the mountains at the head of his troops.

This is a gesture, not quite successful, towards focusing something which the play badly needed to focus. When John talked in Act One about his duty and honour under the open sky in the North, the words were obviously backed by a serious purpose, but the subsequent very amusing changes in the situation made it impossible to gauge just how serious he'd been. A character in a play obviously consists chiefly of the words he speaks but Rupert, though we never saw him in action, was made triumphantly real as a man of action. The character of John Hogarth and the play that contains him are both fascinating but both finally too vague because they're both too much a matter of words.

THE DEVILS

After the richly undeserved failures of his three major plays and after *The Gates of Summer* failed to reach London, Whiting gave up the theatre for the cinema. He'd been doing some work on treatments and dialogue since 1952 and his first screenplay was *The Ship that Died of Shame* (1954) from the story by Nicholas Monsarrat. He also rewrote *The Good Companions* (1956), wrote *Talk of the Devil* (1956), collaborated with Bryan Forbes on *The Captain's Table* (1957), did some revisions on *Cleopatra*, some work with Christopher Fry on *The Bible* and eight other full screenplays.

It was Peter Hall who enticed him back into the theatre. Peter Hall had been an ardent admirer right from the beginning. When he was still at Cambridge he did an excellent production of *Saint's Day* at the A.D.C. Theatre in November 1952, with Tony Church as Paul, and a delightful *Penny for a Song* in the summer of 1953. He commissioned *No Why* for the Arts Theatre, and in 1960, as director of the Royal Shakespeare Company, he approached Whiting to write a large scale costume drama for their first season at the Aldwych. Whiting proposed an adaptation of either Aldous Huxley's *The Devils of Loudun* or Frederick Rolfe's *Hadrian VII*. *The Devils* was produced in February 1961, but though it was to be much more successful than any of his earlier plays, the production suffered from Whiting's normal bad luck. On the first night Patrick Allen (d'Armagnac) had to duck to avoid having his hat knocked off by an arch which was being flown in and Richard Johnson (Grandier) was suffering from laryngitis. He got through the performance but he wasn't in good form and his understudy had to take over on the second night.

The Devils is a very good play but Whiting's genius didn't work at its best when he wasn't creating his own characters. Paul and Rupert are both conceptions who get crystallized into their theatrical existence out of a solution in which a very complex chemical interaction has taken place. The curve of their on-stage lives is an exact rendering of something that Whiting was burning to say and issues of great current importance are reflected and refracted in every facet of the crystal. *Saint's Day* is not primarily *about* the relationship between the artist and society and *Marching Song* is not primarily a play *about* conscience and 'democracy' catching up with a Nazi general. If you had to say what the plays were about, you'd have to say that they were both about men who rose out of the ranks of ordinariness, became less human in the process and, much too late, underwent a conversion when they came to understand the losses involved in what they'd gained. When he was free to choose his own raw material, and not adapting someone else's, Whiting invented stage action which was complete and satisfying in itself and through which a vast amount could be said, both directly and indirectly. But unlike Brecht's and Shakespeare's, his talent for creating wasn't coupled with an equal talent for adapting.

Aldous Huxley's book *The Devils of Loudun* doesn't quite succeed in integrating all its material. Even if he'd limited himself to the historical subject matter, Huxley would have had a hard time making the separate stories of Soeur Jeanne, Grandier and Surin coalesce, for the exorcist didn't come on to the scene until after Grandier's execution, and one of the main points of the story is the disconnection of its elements. The only contact Grandier ever had with the nuns of the Ursuline convent was a negative one: he turned down an invitation to be their director. But he was unlucky. He was good-looking and proud, enjoyed making love, couldn't help making enemies. He got the daughter of the Public Prosecutor pregnant and abandoned her. Following the example of their neurasthenic Mother Superior, the nuns started dreaming about him, having visions, becoming hysterical, producing symptoms of what was taken to be diabolical possession and, encouraged by the exorcists, they denounced Grandier as a magician. Richelieu was on the side of his enemies and he was imprisoned, tried, and burned at the stake. The number of coincidences Grandier had working against him would alone make the story difficult to tell coherently. Quite naturally Huxley was fascinated by such ghastly examples of cruelty, by the appalling behaviour of the clerics and laymen who acted in the name of God and the Church against all reason in venting their spite on a man who was completely innocent of what he was accused and whose innocence was quite apparent to many contemporary observers. But Huxley's main interest is in using the story as a stalking horse. His real subject is self-transcendence. He claims that 'an urge to self-transcendence is almost as widespread and at times almost as powerful as the urge to self-assertion'. The 'insulated self' is a prison from which various escapes are possible. Saints and mystics have succeeded in escaping upwards into spirituality, striving towards a 'union with the spirit which links the Unknown to the known'. There are also downward and horizontal escapes 'into subhuman or merely human substitutes for Grace'. Horizontal transcendence is the most common: Huxley uses the term rather vaguely to mean 'identification with a cause wider than one's own immediate interest' and he includes business, marriage, hobbies and scientific research in the category. The downward escape routes include alcohol, drugs, mass-hysteria and sexual debauchery.

The argument very soon becomes muddy. When he is actually explaining the behaviour of the frantic nuns in terms of sexual starvation, fantasy, mass hysteria and a patient–doctor relationship with the exorcist, in which symptoms are obligingly provided to accord with the diagnosis, Huxley is plausible and persuasive. But many of his psychological generalizations founder on his vagueness about what the 'self' is. Are the impulses that drive the mystic to mysticism and the drunkard to drink external to the self? If debauched sexuality, business activities, and hobbies are all examples of self-transcendence, what is self-assertion?

Whiting leaves out all these psychological generalizations (as he leaves out Surin), but his play isn't uninfluenced by them. Paul and Rupert are both heroes of Huxleyan self-transcendence and Grandier attempts escape routes both upward and downward. The figure of the Sewerman both embodies and expresses a revulsion against the animal facts of human existence, not dissimilar from that expressed by Cadmus.

> SEWERMAN: Every man is his own drain. He carries his main
>   sewer with him. Gutters run about him to carry off the dirt —
> GRANDIER: They also carry the blood of life.
> SEWERMAN: Mere plumbing. Elementary sanitation. Don't
>   interrupt. And what makes a man happy? To eat, and set

the drains awash. To sit in the sun and ferment the rubbish.
To go home, and find comfort in his wife's conduit. Then
why should I feel ashamed or out of place down here?

Cadmus talks of sitting on a dunghill; the Sewerman works in the
sewers. Whiting and Huxley shared a fastidiousness which made
them want to separate out the more animal elements – or the merely
human elements – and they were both deeply interested in the
question of what differentiates the great man from the ordinary
man. Twenty-one years before *The Devils of Loudun* was published,
Huxley had taken a figurative interest in the question of possession,
writing *à propos* of Clémenceau 'A great man differs from ordinary
men in being possessed, as it were, by more than human spirits.'

Whiting was conscious of unresolved ambiguities in his own
position, as he shows by making his characters pose questions like
these:

NINON: I saw you that day just as a man. What's the matter?
GRANDIER: I wish words like that could still hurt me. (*He is
putting scent on his handkerchief.*)
NINON: I've never seen you as anything but a man. Do you
want to be more?
GRANDIER: Of course. Or less.
NINON: But how can you be a man of God without being a
man? . . .

MANNOURY: This human head fills me with anticipation, my
dear Adam.
ADAM: It's a common enough object.
MANNOURY: Every man wears one on his shoulders, certainly.
But when a head comes into my hands disassociated from the
grosser parts of the body I always feel an elevation of spirit.
Think, this is the residence of reason.

But is he not perhaps too schematic in dividing up his characters into
men who are men but try to be more and men who are less than men
and are therefore hostile to the heroes? In *Marching Song* Whiting
held an effective balance between Rupert (who is admirable in so
many ways) and Harry (who is right in so many ways). In *The Devils*
the minor characters are taken from history filtered through Huxley

81

and therefore seen very much more from outside. We see why Adam and Mannoury are so hostile to Grandier. Quite apart from his mockery of them, they're jealous of him because they're less attractive and successful with women. But as characters, unlike Harry, they are totally unsympathetic. The historical episode is one in which almost everyone behaved disgracefully: the play therefore is one with a large cast of villains.

Structurally it differs from all his previous plays more than any of them had differed from the others. It's written much more like a film, with short scenes, a mass of hurriedly sketched minor characters and quick changes of location. He no longer bases his plot on action embedded in the past and he dispenses with the claustrophobic insulation which had always been important before. The house in *Saint's Day* is almost in a state of siege and cut off from the village almost as the island is from the mainland in Strindberg's *The Dance of Death*. In *A Penny for a Song* the look-out in the tree, the gate which shuts out the cannon balls and the very peaceful way everyone prepares for war make sthe Bellboys' garden into a microcosm of English insularity. In *Marching Song* Cadmus's order that no one is allowed to leave the house or come into it makes it into an effective prison. There's less claustrophobia in *The Gates of Summer*, which splits its action between the house and the garden but again we feel marooned away from the city and the main tension depends on whether John will ever escape to the North. In all these plays, great atmosphere exudes from the locale and some of it depends on the set, which is always described meticulously. In *The Devils* there's very little help from the set. In a film it would be very easy to move about the streets of Loudun, from Ninon's bedroom to Trincant's house and away to Poitiers and Paris, but in the theatre the only hope for any designer to give sufficient indication of locale without cluttering the production with incessant changes of set would be by a very clever use of back-projections or Brechtian titles, or perhaps both. In Sean Kenny's set, we were often uncertain of where a particular piece of action was meant to be situated.

The scene with Richelieu talking to Louis XIII in Paris while Grandier talks to d'Armagnac in Loudun was clear enough because we're oriented by d'Armagnac's line

Richelieu sits with the King in Paris. He whispers in his ear.

But the transition from the room in the convent to the market stall is almost impossible to stage. After a soliloquy Jeanne opens a window and sees Grandier in full canonicals, magnificently making his way through the market below. She cries out and, hearing her, he stops, thinking that the cry of agony came from someone in the bustling crowd. With Dorothy Tutin only a few yards away from Richard Johnson, the moment went for nothing, and it's an important one, because this is the only time Jeanne actually sees Grandier until just before his execution, when every hair has been shaved from his head. Sean Kenny and Peter Wood (the director) failed to make it clear what their relative positions were meant to be, but Whiting, thinking now more in cinematic than in stage terms, was certainly making their tasks almost impossible for them.

The sudden appearance of the Bishop of Poitiers is also very confusing for an audience. Absorbed in his pursuit of the theme of self-transcendence, Whiting has very little thought for the difficulties we have in adjusting to a new scene in a new town and a new character who immediately launches into a long speech which starts like this:

> I have been alone for many days now. You will want to know if I have found some kind of grace. Perhaps, for I am filled with weariness and disgust at the folly and wickedness of mankind. Is this the beneficence of God, you ask? It may well be. Let me tell you the circumstances of the revelation.
>
> Shut in my room for seven days, fasting and at prayer, I came to see myself as the humble instrument of God's will. It was a state of such happiness, such bliss, and such abasement that I wished never to return to you. I longed for this husk to wither away, leaving only the purity of spirit. But my sense of duty as your bishop forced me to leave this paradise. I came back to the world.

The contrast between the long literary speeches and the telegraphically terse lines of colloquial dialogue is greater than ever before.

MANNOURY: Well, we have had a nice talk.

John Whiting

ADAM: Have we got anywhere?
MANNOURY: Somebody at the door.
ADAM: Can't be.
MANNOURY: Is.
(ADAM *opens the door.* LAUBARDEMONT *stands there.*)
ADAM: No business. Shut.

There is an example of an abrupt cut from quickfire dialogue to leisurely narrative in this scene between the two exorcists.

RANGIER: Is he among you?
BARRE: Incessantly.
RANGIER: Can we name him?
BARRE: If you want to. Satan.
RANGIER: How is the struggle?
BARRE: I shan't give up.
RANGIER: You look tired.
BARRE: It goes on day and night.
RANGIER: Your spirit is shining.
BARRE: Unbroken, at any rate. But there's never a moment's peace at Chinon now. Only the other day I was conducting a marriage. Everything was going very well. I had before me a young couple, ignorant, I thought, but pure. It never entered my head that they were anything else. I'd reached the blessing, and was about to send them out to the world as man and wife, when there was a disturbance at the west door. A cow had come into the church, and was trying to force its way through the congregation. I knew at once, of course.

But Whiting is very skilful in establishing characters and situations economically. As Adam and Mannoury start spying on Grandier, they become a means of narrating his movements at the same time as revealing their jealousy and their activity in building up a cabal against him. And in one soliloquy, Sister Jeanne tells us a great deal about herself:

I dedicate myself humbly to Your service. You have made me, both in stature and in spirit, a little woman. And I have a small imagination, too. That is why, in Your infinite wisdom, You have given me this visible burden on my back to remind me day by day of what I must carry. O my dear Lord, I find it difficult to turn in my bed, and so in the small and desperate hours I am reminded of Your burden, the Cross, on the long road ... Please God, take away my hump so that I can lie on my back without lolling my head. (*Silence*.) There is a way to be found. May the light of Your eternal love . . . (*whispers*). Amen.

If *The Gates of Summer* followed on too directly and dependently from the earlier plays, *The Devils* is too divorced from them. It's only occasionally that we get echoes, as with the Sewerman's bird, which is reminiscent of Rupert's misunderstanding of the goat-song.

GRANDIER: Do you carry it for love?
SEWERMAN: An idea which would only occur to a good man. Or one careless with hope. No, I carry the thing so that it may die, and I live. He's my saviour. Who's yours?

This exchange takes place immediately after Grandier performs a secret midnight wedding ceremony in the church between Philippe and himself. She is to be his life-line, his means of horizontal self-transcendence, for she gives him

Hope of coming to God by way of a fellow being. Hope that the path, which taken alone, in awful solitude, is a way of despair, can be enlightened by the love of a woman. I have come to believe that by this simple act of committal, which I have done with my heart, it may be possible to reach God by way of happiness.

There is Whiting rhetoric of the old kind in Grandier's speech about secluded women.

Imagine being awakened in the night by a quite innocent dream. A dream of your childhood, or of a friend not seen for many years, or even the vision of a good meal. Now, this is a sin. And so you must take up your little whip and scourge your body. We call that discipline. But pain is sensuality, and in its vortex spin images of horror and lust. My beloved Sister in Jesus seems to have fixed her mind on me. There is no reason, De Cerisay. A dropped handkerchief, a scribbled note, a piece of gossip. Any of these things found in the desert of mind and body caused by continual prayer can bring hope. And with hope comes love. And, as we all know, with love comes hate. So I possess this woman. God help her in her terror and unhappiness.

John Whiting

Though here, more than before, clipped sentences are incorporated into the long speech.

When his attempts at horizontal self-transcendence fail, as Philippe becomes pregnant and he abandons her, Whiting's Grandier, unlike Huxley's, and history's, turns to self-destruction.

> GRANDIER: All worldly things have a single purpose for a man of my kind. Politics, power, the senses, pride, and authority. I choose them with the same care that you, sir, select a weapon. But my intention is different. I need to turn them against myself.
>
> D'ARMAGNAC: To bring about your end?
>
> GRANDIER: Yes. I have a great need to be united with God. Living has drained the need for life from me. My exercise of the senses has flagged to total exhaustion. I am a dead man, compelled to live.

This links him with Whiting's other self-destructive heroes and it ought to make him more interesting than a passive victim when there are urges inside him that join forces with his enemies, but nothing is done dramatically to establish his world-weariness. In the farewell scene with Philippe, he seemed cold, detached, sorry to lose the pleasures of love-making with her but not guilty or suicidal. Then in the next scene in which he appears, we get an explicit statement that the whole intention of the affair with Philippe was self-destructive, which certainly wasn't the way he saw it at the time, according to the evidence Whiting gave us.

The next jump after this is to the speech about creating God, and once again, the change in Grandier is neither substantiated nor integrated dramatically. It's created entirely through the rhetoric of the speech which describes it:

> I created Him from the light and the air, from the dust of the road, from the sweat of my hands, from gold, from filth, from the memory of women's faces, from great rivers, from children, from the works of man, from the past, the present, the future, and the unknown. I caused Him to be from fear and despair. I gathered in everything from this mighty act, all I have known, seen, and experienced. My sin, my presumption, my vanity, my love, my hate, my lust. And last I gave myself and

so made God. And He was magnificent. For He is all these things.

I was utterly in His presence. I knelt by the road. I took out the bread and the wine. *Panem vinum in salutis consecramus hostiam.* And in this understanding He gave Himself humbly and faithfully to me, as I had given myself to Him.

This is the closest Whiting's Grandier can get to upward self-transcendence, but coming right after it, Grandier's arrest outside his own church is too obviously theatrical. But there's a good verbal link between Grandier's big speech and the comfort Father Ambrose is later to give him in the cell. God is here. Christ is now.

AMBROSE: Offer God pain, convulsion, and disgust.
GRANDIER: Yes. Give Him myself.
AMBROSE: Let Him reveal Himself in the only way you can understand.
GRANDIER: Yes! Yes!
AMBROSE: It is all any of us can do. We live a little while, and in that little while we sin. We go to Him as we can. All is forgiven.

In between these two scenes, Jeanne has come as close as a nun could to Procathren's position at the end of *Saint's Day.*

We do not mock our beloved Father in Heaven. Our laughter is kept for His wretched and sinful children who get above their station, and come to believe they have some other purpose in this world than to die.
After the delusions of power come the delusions of love. When men cannot destroy they start to believe they can be saved by creeping into a fellow human being. And so perpetuating themselves. Love me, they say over and over again, love me. Cherish me. Defend me. Save me. They say it to their wives, their whores, their children, and some to the whole human race. Never to God. These are probably the most ridiculous of all, and most worthy of derision. For they do not understand the glory of mortality, the purpose of man: loneliness and death.

The attitude of the other nuns never becomes clear. They listen to her in scenes like this and they follow her lead in the ventriloquist act they do with devils' voices in the exorcism scene but whereas Arthur

John Whiting

Miller in *The Crucible* shows exactly how Abigail keeps the other girls in line, Whiting ignores that question. But he lets the homosexual prince de Condé speak out his disgust against women in general to the painted boys who surround him:

> These are women, darling. Look well. Vomit, if you wish. Man is born of them. Gross things. Nasty. Breeding ground. Eggs hatch out in hot dung. Don't wrinkle your little nose, pet. Take this scent. Some men love them. The priest, Grandier, for example. He's picked the gobbets from the stew. He's —
> (DE CONDÉ *whispers in the boy's ear. The child's eyes widen.* DE CONDÉ *laughs.*)

De Condé's visit to the Loudun scene is historical but the trick he plays in freeing Jeanne from the devils with an empty box, by saying that it contains a phial of Christ's blood, is taken from an episode which involved another visiting nobleman.

> The box was applied to the head of one of the nuns, who immediately exhibited all the symptoms of intense pain and threw a fit. Much delighted, the good friar returned the box to its owner, who thereupon opened it and revealed that, except for a few cinders, it was completely empty. 'Ah, my lord,' cried the exorcist, 'what sort of a trick have you played upon us?' 'Reverend Father,' answered the nobleman, 'what sort of a trick have you been playing upon *us*?'

Whiting uses these lines almost exactly as Huxley quotes them.

The scenes in which De Laubardemont tries to extract a confession from Grandier don't quite measure up to the equivalent scenes in *The Crucible* and it's impossible to do justice on the stage to Huxley's vivid account of the torture and the execution itself, with Grandier remaining calm and dignified while vindictive Capuchins set fire to the straw before the executioner can carry out his promise to strangle the poor parish priest before the flames reach him. But Whiting is very successful in evoking the charnel-house atmosphere in the town after the burning, with Adam and Mannoury talking like two concentration camp doctors about human fat rendered down by heat to the consistency of candle wax while d'Armagnac and de Cerisay drunkenly talk about seeing couples fornicating in the street and an old woman with human remains in a basket. He also does well to end with the Sewerman snatching one of Grandier's charred bones from the men who are fighting for them and offering it to Jeanne.

> They want it to cure their constipation or their headache, to have it bring back their virility or their wife. They want it for love or hate. Do you want it for anything?

NO WHY *AND* A WALK IN
THE DESERT

When Peter Hall commissioned *No Why* in the summer of 1957, he intended it to be a curtain-raiser for Whiting's translation of Anouilh's *The Traveller without Luggage*, but instead of using it when he finally produced the Anouilh at the Arts in January 1959, he got Whiting to translate Anouilh's *Madame De . . . No Why* was published in the *London Magazine* and produced as a radio play by Martin Esslin but it never got staged until July 1964 when John Schlesinger directed it as part of a programme of one-act plays, *Expeditions One*, at the Aldwych.

It's Whiting's least naturalistic play, a piece about a boy locked up in an attic. One by one the members of his family urge him to confess to a crime and ask their forgiveness for it. We're never told what it is, none of them saw him do it and in any case it has very little to do with what they really have against him – the fact that he exists and that he isn't one of them. That he is different from them seems to be a criticism of the phoney values of the society they represent. He never speaks and his silence encourages this impression, as it forces them to go on talking. They talk about being fair, happiness, goodness, having fun, caring, saying prayers, understanding, the beauty of love, being wicked and repenting, making sacrifices, living for others, freedom and justice but his silence becomes a screen on which they project their own guilt. Like Edward and Flora in Pinter's play *A Slight Ache* who can't help giving more and more of themselves away as they talk on into the void created by the match-seller's silence, all the characters in *No Why* show themselves up as they talk to Jacob. The boy was conceived out of carelessness, the plans his parents made for him were motivated by their own anxiety and selfishness, the prison-visiting aunt is as hard as the judge-like old grandfather, the cousin is glib and hypocritical and they're all despicably self-righteous. But the child is defenceless against the unpitying way they invoke goodness to plume themselves and victimize him. In the end, the father takes away even his son's sense of his own identity. Locking him up in the attic for the night, he says he'll come back in the morning

> And then I shall hope to find my real little boy.

It's curious how clearly *No Why* anticipates *The Devils* in the way it shows evil masquerading as goodness and a group representative of society joining forces to crush a weak but stubborn scapegoat who refuses to give them the confession they want. Even the arguments they use are similar to De Laubardemont's when he goes all out to extract a confession from Grandier and we're made to feel that like De Laubardemont they must at some level be aware of the falseness of their own positions and must need the reassurance of a 'confession' from the outsider who isn't actually criticizing them, except implicitly, by not being like them.

It's even possible that Whiting was influenced by *The Devils of Loudun* when he wrote *No Why*. Grandier was shut up in an attic while his enemies were preparing to destroy him and De Laubardemont, who badly needed a confession to silence his critics, went whole-heartedly along with the exorcists' wilful misreading of the evidence in front of their eyes. When Grandier was serene, it was because Satan was hardening his heart, when he spoke of his love for God, he meant the Devil and his professed hatred of the Devil was actually hatred of God. The fact that Jacob was found sitting up in bed eating jelly and drinking milk is counted against him and when Sarah is asked whether she saw the actual crime, she says certainly not, she wouldn't look, she always keeps things nice.

> ELEANOR: Then how did you know it was so bad?
> SARAH (*shouting*): I read the newspapers, don't I? I know what a man is! (*She points at* JACOB.) That! It ought not to be allowed!

Jacob's basic crime is that he's human. As yet, he's rather less than a man, but so are his persecutors.

A Walk in the Desert, a sixty-minute play for television, written in 1959, is Whiting's only piece since *Conditions of Agreement* which suffers from diffuseness. It has some good writing in it, but much of it is pedestrian, partly perhaps because he was insecure in the

John Whiting

medium and took excessive care to get his main points across to the audience, even at the cost of repeating them. He called the play a rewrite of *Conditions of Agreement* but it's hard to see much in common between the two scripts, except that Peter, like Nicholas, is lame, that they're both set in provincial cities, that they both deal with moods of violent bitterness and depression and destructiveness which is mainly aimed against the self.

It's a play without a hero. Even in *No Why*, Jacob's silence becomes more or less heroic but in *A Walk in the Desert* Peter falls short of being a man and his friend Tony though less anti-life in his outlook, has 'given up'. Still unmarried at thirty-six and liable now to be taken for a welfare officer if he goes to the local dances, he doesn't much mind who he spends his time with, contentedly coasting along on a mild vicarious enjoyment of other people's experiences. The father, ultra-serious about his amateur acting, is sympathetic but stupid, while the mother is well-meaning but ineffectual.

After a very slow start we get a protracted exploitation of a practical joke Peter plays on a girl who turns up at the house. She's after a job which is being offered by the successful writer who lives next door. Peter is jealous of him and feels hostile towards the girl as soon as he sees her because she obviously hasn't given up. So he interviews her without telling her she's in the wrong house. She's still trying to 'better' herself and a genuine tension is rather belatedly built up when he pitches hard into her, undermining her values, deriding the district she lives in and scoffing at the chances of ever marrying now that she has an illegitimate child.

It was a soldier who made her pregnant and it was when Peter was in the army that a truck ran over his legs. Both her meeting with her lover and Peter's accident are reconstructed in detail in the familiar style of reviving episodes from the past.

In her resilient hopefulness, Shirley is diametrically unlike Peter but in another sense they're similar, 'eruptions on the smooth face of society' as Peter puts it. And, excluded from that society, an involuntary exile who lives right in the middle of it, he hates it passionately.

> We bring, with our hot drink, the tranquillity of death into life. But there are people like us to ruin this vision. The

welfare schemes and help in the home try to soothe us out of
existence. More is being done every day. The prisons and
mental homes get bigger and safer. There is a place for the
bastard and a place for the sinner. Kindness is now an official
state. It wears a uniform and badges. But where is ordinary
human kindness. The thing which passes between men
without thought. The kindness of love. For you know perfectly
well that no one has given you that sort of kindness. Your
father. You say he was good to you, but you only say that
because you wish he had been. Really, he's ashamed of you.
Remember? Your friends. You haven't got any friends. You
can't cart the baby to the palais on Saturday night and so you
stay away. Now you pretend you're going to start all over
again. You can't. The job, the money won't alter a thing.
You're done for. Like me. Down the High Street we go, you
behind your pram and me shuffling and swaying like a drunkard. The wrongdoer and the wronged. Both of us insults to the
present perfect way of life.

SHIRLEY: He's right, of course. I do pretend. It seemed the
only thing. I'm on my own all right, because of what I did.
More on my own than any person should ever be. And he
means it'll never be different. He's right. This is it. My lot, as
Dad says. For always.

But the tension is only sustained until Shirley finds out the truth
and resentfully goes away. There's one good scene when Tony, after
watching through the window as Shirley is turned away from the
house next door, forces Peter to say why he treated her so badly.
Peter explains it in terms of a compulsion to make himself felt. But
the rest of the play leans heavily on the kind of contrived suspense
that's all too familiar in television plays. When Peter's parents come
back early from the amateur theatricals, we hear that 'something
funny' has happened outside. The facts build up to suggest that Shirley
might have drowned herself. A passing ambulance bell is heard and
the mother has seen policemen up to their waists in water. Then Shirley
releases the tension by coming back for the handbag she's left behind
and announcing that the police have been rescuing a stray cat.

The play ends with a very depressed monologue from Peter. He's
in conversation with his father but the old man doesn't say anything

and doesn't understand much of what's being said, except that in some way he's being rejected. Peter talks about the isolation he feels, as if he were in a wilderness. The speech is accompanied by pictures on the screen of Shirley and Tony on their way away from Peter, of the rainswept town square, of a train leaving from the station, of a deserted by-pass road. Images of desolation.

'NO TIME FOR TRAGEDY'

In 1961, when he was writing on theatre for the *London Magazine,* Whiting complained about a review of Tynan's in the *Observer* titled 'No Time for Tragedy'. It predicted that 'satire, irony, gallows-humour and other mutations of the comic spirit will be the guiding forces of our theatre in the coming years. Tragedy . . . has little to say to a rebellious generation obsessed by the danger of imminent mega-deaths.' Tynan was certainly right in contending that there was very little contemporary tragedy. He defined tragedy as 'the re-enactment of stories wherein men pass through anguish and are destroyed by forces they neither comprehend nor control'. He was also right in saying – as it had often been said before – that Christianity and Marxism were both inimical to the spirit of tragedy. The Christian faith in divine justice and the Marxist faith in social revolution as a cure for economic injustice both contradict the tragedian's almost religious faith in a hostile fate. The gods are there, but they're unjust. Suffering has nothing to do with punishment. Hamlet and Oedipus may not be faultless, but they don't deserve what happens to them and the something that's rotten in the state of Denmark and in the state of Thebes isn't something that could be put right by a stiff programme of social reforms. In the perspective of tragedy, you see beyond the interrelationships that are subject to human control and the cathartic cleansing that tragic suffering produces, goes beyond the immediate situation. 'Tragedy,' as Susan Sontag has put it, 'is a vision of nihilism, a heroic or ennobling vision of nihilism.'

The basic difference between Tynan's position and Whiting's is summed up in one sentence of Tynan's, 'There is today hardly an aspect of human suffering (outside the realm of medicine) for which politics, psychiatry and environmental psychology cannot offer at least a *tentative* solution.' Whiting believed that life was lived – and always had been lived – on a tragic level. He wasn't insensitive to his social and economic environment, but he wasn't content to interpret human experience purely in social and economic terms. He vigorously rejected the assumption that man is capable of moulding his own destiny, which Tynan describes as '*the idée reçue* of modern drama'. It's conducive to comedy and for Tynan, comedy was quite capable of filling the space vacated by tragedy. Beckett and Ionesco employ farcical devices to express a view of life as grimly deterministic as any Greek's'. The plays he best remembered from Theatre Workshop and the Royal Court were all comic on one level or another and the death of Arthur Miller's salesman wasn't tragic, for the play's 'catastrophe depends entirely on the fact that the company Willy Loman works for has no pensions scheme for its employees'.

But *Saint's Day* and *Marching Song* are heroic and ennobling views of nihilism. Whiting isn't the only nihilist among contemporary playwrights but he's the only one to be so religious in his outlook, so much a moralist and so much a theatrical poet. He was not only interested in religion: he was compelled to include – or at least to imply – God's empty throne in his panorama of godless men. He was interested in what it meant to be a man and to study this in a theatrical perspective, you have to see the empty spaces around the man-made problems and relationships – man in relationship not just with other men but with the totality of his existence. You find – if you didn't know all the time – that there are aspects of human suffering (quite outside the realm of medicine) to which politics, psychiatry and environmental psychology are quite irrelevant.

It was the moralist in Whiting, his constant concern with right and wrong, which made him project on to his heroes a carefully balanced mixture of good and bad characteristics. It's not simply a question of whether they behave well or badly. Characters who behave exactly like this could have been made far more sympathetic, but by highlighting their unsympathetic sides, Whiting, perhaps consciously, discouraged empathy. Which is bad for box-office business.

But what distinguishes Rupert from any other modern hero created by any other modern playwright is that he emerges as a great man. Several historical characters – Brecht's Galileo, Eliot's Becket, Bolt's Sir Thomas More – convince us as being great, because they incorporate into their characters features, actions and even some of the language of their prototypes. And, in Becket's case, because of the poetry Eliot puts into his mouth. But in an original character it's extremely hard to create genius or greatness. Whiting succeeds partly because of the poetry in his prose, partly because of the poetry in his situations. The atmosphere contributes to the heightening effect and the language Rupert speaks lifts him above the level of the *homme moyen sensuel*. We get larger-than-lifesize heroes in Brecht, Tennessee Williams, John Osborne, Montherlant, Anouilh and a dozen others, but they are not tragic heroes, even if they pass through anguish or are destroyed by forces they neither comprehend nor control. In a period when tragedy was thought to be dead and critics like George Steiner and Lionel Abel have written elaborate funeral orations, Whiting has quietly revived the corpse.

Like Huxley, Whiting was passionately interested in what the forces were that raised some men above the level of the rest, but he was equally interested in the common multiples. But he needed a heroic yardstick to measure the ordinary inch of humanity. Paul and Rupert both have to become much bigger than ordinary men before they can realize how inadequate they are and they have to cut themselves right off from the human herd before they can feel a strong urge to come back into it.

It's a phenomenal feat of playwriting to make the self-destruction in *Saint's Day* as heroic and ennobling as it is. The society which Paul rejects is corrupt – and Whiting fills our nostrils with a stench that doesn't come just from the village – but Paul's rejection also reflects on himself. We never know quite to what extent his exile was self-imposed; we do know that by choosing silence he has opted out of his responsibilities, escaping into fantasy. He acts irresponsibly in bringing Robert face to face with death, with the void. Robert gets his revenge but he has to take the responsibility for his irresponsible action in doing so. If death is what life is about, killing and dying are ways of exploring it to the full. Neither Paul's withdrawal into unreality nor Robert's action in killing him are intrinsically heroic but, like Rupert, like John Hogarth and like Grandier, Robert commits himself totally by his final action, and is willing to take the consequences. Together, Paul and Robert make a composite hero. Each wears the other's hubris turned inside out and the effect of the sacrifice is cathartic. There's even a hint of regeneration in the end of the play as the child dances with the green scarf.

97

John Whiting

Marching Song is a more classical play and Rupert is a less equivocal hero who has distinguished himself in the classical way – as a warrior. His strengths and weaknesses are both on the grand scale, as the Harry parallel stresses. Many lesser men would treat Catherine far better than Rupert does but his inability to pretend or compromise shows something of his greatness and the chiaroscuro of the language Whiting puts into his mouth fleshes him out as a hero, though his only positive action in the play is the negative one of self-annihilation. He's not as innocent a sufferer as Oedipus and the play is less explicitly nihilistic than *Saint's Day*. Rupert has chosen his fate in his career: the present prisoner is the victim of the past general and the present suffering only a continuation of the anguish at being unable to go on when he got stuck on the wrong side of the river. But his death is cathartic. Again, Whiting brilliantly packs impressions of a whole society into a single room, and though Rupert is in no sense dying for the people, Dido's final decision to commit herself to Catherine, like the child's dance in *Saint's Day*, contains a strong hint of regeneration.

The reason Whiting's plays are difficult to follow is that so much is packed into them. It's pointless to sneer as Tynan did that 'somewhere in Mr Whiting's imagination there glows a vision of an ideal theatre where the playwright is freed from the necessity of attracting customers, where his fastidious cadences are not tainted by exposure to rank plebeian breath'. Whiting couldn't have written anything like so well if he'd avoided everything that would be hard for an audience to follow. And neither could Shakespeare.